IMPORTANT TELEPHONE NUMBERS

Veterinarian: _____

Address: _____

Telephone: _____

Emergency clinic or
   veterinary hospital: _____

Poison control center: _____

ASPCA (humane shelter): _____

Local bird club: _____

YOUR BIRD'S RECORDS

Name _____ Type _____ Breeder _____

Date of birth _____ Sex _____ Band number _____

Domestic-Raised _____ Imported (Country of Origin _____)

Date Imported _____ Where Purchased _____

New-Bird Exam

Date _____

Physical Exam Results: General condition _____

   Gram Stain: Feces _____ Choane _____

   Culture and Sensitivity _____

   Complete Blood Count (CBC) _____

   Basic Avian Blood Tests _____

   Psittacosis Test: Blood _____ Feces _____

   Fecal _____

   Giardia Test _____

   Radiograph (x-rays) _____

Surgery   **Date**

_____

_____

_____

_____

_____

Date bred	Mate	Number of eggs	How many hatched alive	How many died in shell or within 2 days	Band numbers

Problem or illness	Date	Medication used	Doctor was seen	Used home treatment	Resolved without treatment

Diagnostic Procedures

	Date	Results
Cultures		
Blood tests		
Electrocardiograms		
Radiographs (X-rays)		
Endoscopy		
Biopsy		
Cytology		
Urinalysis		
Fecal		

The
BIRD
CARE
Book
REVISED AND UPDATED

Other Books by
Sheldon L. Gerstenfeld, V.M.D.

The Dog Care Book
The Cat Care Book

Zoo Clues (for children)

The
BIRD
CARE
Book

REVISED AND UPDATED

**All you need to know to keep
your bird healthy and happy**

Sheldon L. Gerstenfeld, V.M.D.

Addison-Wesley Publishing Company, Inc.
Reading, Massachusetts   Menlo Park, California   New York
Don Mills, Ontario   Wokingham, England   Amsterdam   Bonn
Sydney   Singapore   Tokyo   Madrid   San Juan

We gratefully acknowledge the following for permission to reprint previously published material: Page 23: From *Birdy* by William Wharton. Copyright © 1978 by William Wharton. By permission of Alfred A. Knopf, Inc.

Many of the designations used by manufacturers and sellers to distinguish their products are claimed as trademarks. Where those designations appear in this book and Addison-Wesley was aware of a trademark claim, the designations have been printed in initial capital letters (i.e., Ivermectin).

The author and publisher have tried to ensure the accuracy of the information in this book. Readers should nevertheless verify all information with their veterinarians. Neither the publisher nor the author may be held responsible for any damage, direct or indirect, which may be caused or exacerbated by treatment described in this book.

Library of Congress Cataloging-in-Publication Data

Gerstenfeld, Sheldon L., 1943–
    The bird care book / Sheldon L. Gerstenfeld.—Rev. and updated.
      p.   cm.
    Bibliography: p.
    Includes indexes.
    ISBN 0-201-09559-9
    1. Cage birds—Diseases. 2. Cage birds. 3. Birds—Diseases.
  I. Title.
  SF994.2.A1G47   1988
  636.6'86—dc19   88-19290
                                                                 CIP

Cover design by Hannus Design Associates
Cover photo by Adolf Schmidecker/FPG
Text design by Sally Carson, Carson Design
Set in 10-point Cheltenham by Compset, Inc., Beverly, MA

ABCDEFGHIJ-DO-89
First printing, April 1989

To my dear wife, Traudi, and dear son, Tyler,
love always

To my dear grandparents,
Samuel and Rose Gerstenfeld
Samuel and Blanche Weiss

To Mr. H. Bird,
the Hummingbird who touched our lives

Acknowledgments

Many people were responsible for *The Bird Care Book*.

My dear wife, Traudi, made very helpful comments and was a wonderful companion on my bird-related travels.

I want to thank Dr. Sam Weeks and Jennifer Delafield for introducing me to the fascinating world of birds during our beautiful Brigantine, New Jersey, days. Dr. Weeks also contributed generously to the wild bird chapter.

I'd like to thank Dr. Margaret Petrak, who took time from her busy schedule to review the manuscript.

The Association of Avian Veterinarians, a group that I'm very proud to be a member of, deserves special gratitude for its unselfish sharing of experiences and information. Fifty veterinarians attended our first meeting in 1980 in Kalamazoo, Michigan. We now have over 2,000 members around the world!

I would like to thank Dr. Walter Rosskopf and Dr. Richard Woerpel for contributing information on the most frequent medical problems seen in each bird species. Thanks also to Dr. Susan and Kevin Clubb for their baby bird diet.

A special thanks to Greg and Linda Harrison, Bob Altman, and Ted LaFeber— a few of the pioneers, nurturers, movers, and shakers of modern avian medicine.

As always, Lois Hammer transformed my handwritten manuscript into a typewritten beauty.

I also want to thank the General Publishing staff of Addison-Wesley for making my creative side such a positive, joyous experience. I'm so fortunate to have been able to write the text and do my cartoons!

Finally, I want to thank my parents, Sidney and Isabelle, for always believing that anything is possible—if you have faith.

To the Reader

This book can be of great help to you and your bird. Several veterinarians have reviewed the text and have agreed on the medical care suggested for each problem. Nevertheless, the recommendations may not always work. Here are some qualifications for you to bear in mind:

1. If your bird is under the care of a veterinarian who gives advice contrary to that given in the book, follow your veterinarian's advice. Your veterinarian can take into account the individual characteristics of your bird.
2. You know your bird best. If you believe you should seek professional help for your bird for any reason, do so.
3. If you think your bird has or might have an allergy to a medication, call your veterinarian for advice.
4. If your bird's problem persists beyond a reasonable period, make an appointment with your veterinarian.

Contents

Contents

Contents

Preface

Albert Schweitzer said that only through reverence for life can we establish a spiritual and humane relationship with people and all other living creatures within our reach. Throughout history, birds have always represented the beauty and mysteries of life and so have been domesticated and kept in cages for decoration or amusement. Only recently have the physical and mental requirements of caged birds been taken into account.

Owning a bird is a big responsibility. With the information in this book, you will be able to take good care of your bird at home and ensure that professional veterinary care is obtained when necessary.

Most bird illnesses begin with poor management—inadequate nutrition and improper caging. Like all other animals (including humans), birds need contact with other birds (or with patient, understanding humans) for their mental health. A feather-picking, malnourished bird kept in a small cage and deprived of contact with other birds or with humans is a pathetic sight.

The Bird Care Book provides the latest information on birds—selecting the right type, nutrition, housing, medical care, etc. You can save time and money and provide the best care for your bird by learning to treat many of its medical problems at home and by knowing when it is important to visit or telephone your veterinarian. Survival in the wild depends upon hiding illness, and birds in captivity have not lost this ability. Most bird illnesses are treatable if the owner recognizes the warning signs early. The detailed Decision Charts will provide you with enough information to make sound judgments about most of your bird's medical problems.

Part I provides bird owners with much useful information.

Selecting a Bird • Taking care of a bird actually starts *before* you choose one (or two, or more). This chapter will help you select and find the proper bird for your lifestyle. The responsibility of bird ownership is stressed.

The Owner's Home Physical Exam • You'll be fascinated by the re-markable adaptations for flight and survival in your bird's body. This chapter also shows you how to examine your bird at home.

Keeping Your Bird Happy and Healthy • Many bird illnesses and in-juries are the result of poor nutrition, inadequate housing, or carelessness when letting a bird out of its cage. A proper home, good nutrition, exercise, training, and an annual well-bird veterinary visit will keep your bird healthy.

Going to the Veterinarian • Finding a competent and interested veteri-narian and being a cooperative, aware, and concerned owner are important for your bird's health. You should understand and appreciate the procedures your ve-terinarian may follow in diagnosing and properly treating your bird's health problem.

Your Bird's Home Pharmacy and Home Hospital • This chapter will help you stock your bird pharmacy with the most effective medications for minor medical problems. Included are hints on uses, dosages, and possible side effects for a variety of over-the-counter medications. Many bird illnesses can be treated at home in a "home hospital."

In Part II, you can find specific guidance for fifty of the most common medical problems of birds. This section is designed for quick and easy reference. After you identify your bird's primary symptoms (for instance, regurgitation, loose drop-pings, or runny nose), you then look in the contents or the index to find a discus-sion of the problem.

Emergency Procedures • This chapter details the best way to deal with an injured bird and what actions you should take when each minute could mean the difference between life and death.

Accidents and Injuries • Common injuries sustained by birds are thor-oughly discussed, with a list of appropriate home treatments and what to expect from your veterinarian.

Common Problems and Diseases • A detailed look at medical prob-lems is provided. This chapter includes general descriptions, suggestions for home treatment, and pointers on when to telephone and when to visit your veterinarian. The information on what to expect at the veterinarian's office will make you aware of what constitutes appropriate care. The Decision Charts that accompany each problem provide step-by-step instructions to help you decide whether to use home treatment or to seek professional advice. No medication suggested in this section should be used without knowledge of its dosage and side effects. Most medicines are discussed in Chapter 5, "Your Bird's Home Pharmacy." First aid information for handling the most common bird emergencies is provided. A combination of the way you handle the emergency at home and your knowledge of what to expect at the veterinarian's office may save your bird's life. Prevention of injuries and illness is also discussed.

Behavior Problems • This chapter includes a helpful discussion on diagnosing and treating screaming, aggression, and biting.

Breeding Your Bird • Breeding, nest building, egg laying, egg sitting, feeding the "babies," and weaning are fully discussed. Decision Charts on egg laying and the nestling period will give you easy instructions to follow if your help—or the veterinarian's help—is needed. The importance of aviculture and domestic hand raising of birds is also discussed.

Owning a pet bird will whet your appetite for watching wild birds. Part III provides information on feeders and feeding, bathing and drinking facilities, nest sites, nest material, and injuries. Happy bird owning and bird-watching!

Chestnut Hill, Pennsylvania   S.L.G.

The
BIRD
CARE
Book
REVISED AND UPDATED

PART I

You and Your Bird

Selecting a Bird

What would the earth be like if there were no birds?

There probably would be no lush, tropical jungles and few trees and bushes up north. • Such birds as hummingbirds and parrots are important pollinators of flowering trees and shrubs in the tropics, and woodpeckers, crows, jays, pigeons, and thrushes (to name only a few) disperse seeds. According to Joel C. Welty in *Life of Birds,* such activities worked against the enterprising eighteenth-century Dutch settlers on the East Indian island of Amboina. Their efforts to sustain a monopoly of the nutmeg trade were frustrated by fruit pigeons who carried the undigested nutmeg seeds to other islands.

Our agricultural crops would have a tougher time developing. • The world would be overrun with weeds and insects. Owls and hawks keep rodents under control. Hairy woodpeckers and yellow-shafted flickers eat those insects that are harmful to our agricultural crops. Sparrows have a large appetite for weed seeds, grasshoppers, and beetles. Not *all* birds help the farmer. Some eat "good" insects such as the cross-pollinating bees. Blackbirds seem to find the Arkansas rice fields tasty.

The beautiful literature and art related to birds would not exist. •

> Teach us, sprite or bird,
>   What sweet thoughts are thine:
> I have never heard
>   Praise of love or wine
> That panted forth a flood of rapture so divine.
> . . . Teach me half the gladness
>   That thy brain must know,
> Such harmonious madness
> From my lips would flow
> The world should listen then, as I am listening now!
>   Percy Bysshe Shelley, *To a Skylark*

There wouldn't be John Keats's *Ode to a Nightingale,* Thomas Hardy's *The Darkling Thrush,* Edgar Allan Poe's *The Raven,* and William Wharton's *Birdy.*
There wouldn't be any John Gould or Audubon drawings and paintings.

We would not have "reached for the heavens." • Airplanes, space travel and exploration, satellites, and global communication—all of these can be linked to birds and the dream of flight they inspired.

There would be no birdkeeping or birdwatching. • Who was the first birdkeeper? Was it Noah? He was supposed to take a male and female of every *flying,* walking, and creeping thing on earth.

Birds in history. The ancient sport of falconry originated about 2000 B.C. in China. At about the same time in Egypt, birds were brought back from expeditions and displayed in the royal zoo. Alexander the Great brought back parrots and peacocks from his conquests in India. The ancient Romans brought back parrots as souvenirs from their African trips. The parrot was so beloved as a pet that it even accompanied the Romans on their conquests.

The Renaissance saw a boom in the aviaries that complemented the beautiful walled gardens in Europe. In the mid-1500s, the Spanish and Portuguese introduced Europe to the canaries from the Canary Islands. The enchantment with the canary's songs and colors continues today.

The parrot seemed to be a prize of conquests. A pair of Cuban Amazon parrots were brought home to Barcelona by Columbus and presented to Queen Isabella. Parrots were also very popular during the Renaissance and admired, as they are today, for their brilliant colors and their ability to mimic the human voice.

The European bird cages from the 1300s on were very ornate, sometimes made of gold and garnished with emeralds, sapphires, pearls, and other precious stones. Although they were visually beautiful, such cages were inhumane, being too short and narrow for comfortable flights.

Roller canaries were very popular in the 1820s. In fact, these songbirds were even "hired" as attractions at balls. The cages were grouped at the foot of the stairway, and as the guest of honor entered, the covers were removed and the guest was greeted with a fanfare of birdsong.

John Gould brought the first budgerigars to England in 1840 from Australia. They were extremely popular and remain so today.

Canary clubs took wing in the 1840s. Beginning in 1890, bird shows became very popular in England and as a result brought a lot of birds in close contact, which caused bird diseases to flourish. An active interest in bird health and nutrition began at this time.

History repeats itself. In ancient Rome, parrots sometimes accompanied their masters to the battlefront. During World War II, pet canaries were known to accompany their masters into battle.

Birdkeeping, especially budgerigar owning, reached "boom" proportions between 1950 and 1965. Today bird clubs, bird shows, and bird ownership are gaining a new popularity. In fact, interest in the health and well-being of pet birds has resulted in a special interest group of veterinarians—the Association of Avian Veterinarians.

Birdwatching

Blue jays and chickadees were "guests" of Thoreau at Walden Pond in the winter of 1845. Pre-Columbian Indians hung hollow gourds in their villages as nesting sites for purple martins. Humans have always delighted in watching birds fly and listening to their song. Birds provide a link with other places, with the past and the future, and with the change of seasons. Who has not marveled at their nest-building skills? Who has not become saddened when geese fly above in their traditional V formations, signalling the end of summer and the beginning of the cold, grey, northern winter?

Today birdwatching is a national pastime. Millions are caring for the birds in their gardens or getting out in the fields to observe birds. Many amateur birdwatchers are contributing vital information about bird migration and habits. Birds are part of the chain of all living things. By studying them, we understand ourselves better. From a conservationist's viewpoint, what affects birds also affects us.

BECOMING AN OWNER

Birds have always been found in and around our homes. Although bird owning has been popular in the past, the *welfare* of these pets has not been considered. Birds were kept in ornate cages that were much too small and did not allow for social contact. Our pet birds have been malnourished because of improper diet. Birds are *social* animals. They thrive on contact with other birds or with caring, gentle humans. Their mental and physical health deteriorates if they receive little or no social contact.

I saw a very sad sight a few years ago—a budgerigar unhappily sitting on a perch in a cage in which it could not even turn around. Its tail feathers were completely frayed from rubbing on the bars. The bird had no companionship—bird or human. It died the day after I saw it. Its sad one-year existence was over. I'll always remember the plight of that bird. In this book, I hope to impress upon you the importance of making a *home* for living things for which you are taking *responsibility*.

Owning a bird brings joy *and* responsibility. Many owners lack such feelings of responsibility, as can be seen in newspaper ads or in a veterinarian's office: "African grey for sale . . . cheap." Didn't the owners realize such birds live a long time—for sixty to seventy years? Didn't they study the method of training *before* buying the bird? Did the bird become sickly from a poor diet? Did the owners get a "good buy"—possibly a diseased bird that was smuggled into our country?

Many birds illnesses are the result of stress (especially among parrots that are imported) and poor nutrition. As a potential bird owner, you *must* do your homework *before* looking for a bird. You must learn how to select a healthy bird and how to keep it healthy.

Owning a bird means a commitment of time (as much as forty to seventy-five years for the larger parrots) and money.

The life span of the common pet birds varies from three years to more than sixty years:

Finches	5–10 years
Canaries	10–20 years
Budgerigars	10–20 years
Cockatiels	10–20 years
Lovebirds	10–20 years
African greys	60–70 years
Macaws	60–70 years

As you can see, bird ownership may require a similar time commitment to dog or cat ownership, and owning one of the large parrots may demand the equivalent of a golden wedding anniversary—50 years!

You and your family should ask yourselves the following questions before deciding on the new family member:

Do we have time for a bird? • Who will have the responsibility for feeding the bird and cleaning the cage? (If no one cleans it, *it will smell!*) Who will train the bird? Will we be able to provide for its *mental* health—its social contact needs?

Can we afford to keep a bird healthy and well-nourished? • For the small bird, the purchase price is small change compared to the maintenance fees: food, accessories, and veterinary care. The large birds (such as macaws) have large price tags and are more costly to maintain. They are very expensive birds and should be kept only by the serious, committed owner.

The cost of feeding and caring for a small bird (such as a budgerigar) for one year ranges between $50 to $100 per year, including the initial veterinary visit; larger birds such as parrots may cost as much as $150 to $300 per year. Remember, too, that any new bird must have a complete physical examination at your veterinarian's office to check the bird's general health and discuss the type of care it will require.

What type of bird should I buy? • Most first-time bird owners choose finches, canaries, cockatiels, or budgerigars as their first feathered pet since these birds are relatively inexpensive and easy to care for. The larger parrots should be purchased only by experienced birdkeepers.

Finches, canaries, cockatiels, and budgerigars also make wonderful pets for

BIRD COST-CARE CHART

Bird	Cost	Considerations
Finches	$25–300 (pair)	Easy care
Canaries	Male $60–150 Female $35–75	Easy care Males are more expensive since they are the singers
Budgerigars	$25–100	Easy care
Cockatiels	$75–150	Easy care Easy to train
Lovebirds	$50–100	Not easy to tame or train
Amazons—domestic hand-raised	$800–2,000	Good talkers, especially the double-yellows and yellow-naped Can be screamers
African greys—domestic hand-raised	$1,500–2,000	Wonderful talkers
Macaws—domestic hand-raised	$3,500–7,000 (scarlet, blue, and gold) $6,000–10,000 (hyacinth)	Will talk, but not as avidly as certain Amazons and African greys
Cockatoos—domestic hand-raised	$2,500 (lesser sulphur crested) $2,500–4,000 (moluccan, umbrella, greater sulphur crested)	Known for their beauty and acrobatics rather than their gift of speech

children—but you may well end up caring for and cleaning up after the bird if you do not carefully consider both your schedule and your child's ability to assume responsibility before buying such a pet.

Do we have room for a bird? Can it adapt to our family? • The larger parrots need roomy metal cages and playground areas. Do you have the room? Will the family cat or dog bother the bird?

What are the positive and negative characteristics of the bird? • Discuss this question *before* you purchase the bird with pet-shop owners, bird breeders, a veterinarian who has a special interest in birds, birdkeepers in the zoo, or people in your town who own the type of bird that you like.

What about the noise factor? • If you live in an apartment or if your family members can't tolerate noise, the larger parrots may not be your cup of tea. The squawks may not be music to your neighbors' ears. Out of courtesy, talk to your neighbors and all family members about your intentions.

Is the bird the right pet for our children? • In my experience, most parents end up caring for the bird (or the dog or the cat). Keep this in mind when the family decision is being made.

How about our other pets? • Many dogs and cats can adapt well to having a bird as a new family member, and many birds—especially the parrot-type birds—tolerate and even like the companionship of some dogs and cats.

Do we take a lot of vacations? • Is there someone to care for your bird while you are away?

THE BIRD BUYER'S GUIDE

The best way to purchase a bird is to find a well-nourished, domestic-bred, hand-raised baby, free of all the known diseases that affect that species. Ask your avian veterinarian for a breeder's list. It will be worth it. You will pay more for the bird, but your veterinary bills will most likely be smaller and you will begin with a happy, healthy and people-oriented bird.

Finches

Finches have their own unique songs. If you like a rainbow choice of colors, you'll love finches. Finches thrive in the company of other finches.

The most common medical problems of finches are bacterial infections (page 93), wheezing from air sac mites (page 166), tapeworms (page 138), egg binding (page 95), and dry gangrene of the toes (page 174).

They live five to ten years and weigh ten to fifteen grams.

Canaries

Home for the wild species of canaries is the Canary Islands, Madeira, and the Azores. The canary was introduced to Europe in the sixteenth century. During the last four centuries, they have been bred for specific characteristics of singing ability, feathering, and coloring. Song canaries are either rollers or choppers. A roller sings loudly with its beak nearly closed, whereas the chopper looks like an operatic soprano belting out the high notes with its beak wide open. If you are buying a canary for its singing ability, hear it sing. Males sing much better than females.

Keep canaries in the largest cage that you can afford. Make sure that it is a long cage, because canaries love to exercise.

In general, canaries are healthy birds. Their most common medical problems are bacterial infections (page 93), feather cysts (page 148), baldness in males (page 152), scaly leg mites (pages 97), dry gangrene of the toes (page 174), wheezing from air sac mites (page 166), and egg binding (pages 95).

They live ten to twenty years and weigh fifteen to thirty grams.

Budgerigars

Budgerigars (budgies) are native to the drier areas of Australia and were introduced to England in 1843 by John Gould, the wildlife artist and contemporary of John Audubon. The Lady Gouldian finch was named in honor of him.

Budgies are easily tamed, very friendly, and talkative. They have been known to recite over 380 sentences and 600 words!

On its forehead the immature budgie has dark color bars, which disappear at maturity (four months old). Mature male budgies have blue ceres at the base of their beaks (most of the time), and females have pink or light brown ceres. The cere *can* fool you. Some blue-cered males actually are females!

Budgies have many health problems, some of which seem to be hereditary. They are "tumor factories." Fatty tumors, kidney and sex gland tumors (page 148), scaly face mites (page 97), gout (pages 176), hypothyroidism (page 140), diabetes mellitus (pages 134, 138), bacterial infections (page 93), paralysis of one leg caused by gonad or kidney tumor (page 145), giardiasis (page 68), and fatty livers (page 142) are common.

They live ten to twenty years and weigh thirty to thirty-five grams.

Cockatiels

Cockatiels are lovable and easy to tame, and they are great entertainers. They are highly recommended (as are parakeets) for your first pet bird. Superior whistling makes up for their limited talking ability.

Adult colors are in full bloom at nine to twelve months of age. At four to six months of age yellow appears around the orange cheek patch in males. The females have yellow spots under their wings and bars on the underside of their tails by six months of age.

Typical characteristics of adult cockatiels include the following:

Male	Female
Bright yellow face	Lighter yellow face
Bright yellow crest	Lighter yellow crest
Dark orange cheek spot	Dull orange cheek spot
Underside of tail—dark grey	Yellow spots under wings
	Color bars on underside of tail feathers

The common medical problems of cockatiels include the following: bacterial infections (page 93), psittacosis (pages 69–70), conjunctivitis (mycoplasma) (page 178), giardia (page 68), diabetes (pages 134, 138), feather picking (page 182), lead poisoning (page 126), chronic egg laying, and egg binding (page 95). The gray cockatiel seems to be the healthiest, whereas the hybrids such as the lutinos are weaker, sicker, and short-lived (perhaps because of immune deficiencies).

They live ten to twenty years and weigh eighty to ninety grams.

Lovebirds

Young, *hand-raised* lovebirds are very affectionate. The older birds are difficult to tame. If you are looking for a talking bird, don't get a lovebird. The most popular species—peach-faced, black-masked, and blue-masked—are from Africa.

Lovebirds are susceptible to psittacosis, bacterial and candida infections, feather-loss problems of unknown cause, and egg binding. Sometimes, also, they do not react well to new additions to their cage, weak or sick birds, or new fledglings, which they may attack and kill.

They live ten to twenty years and weigh forty to fifty grams.

Brotogeris Parakeets

The Brotogeris parakeets are very tame and affectionate, especially the grey-cheeked parakeet, but they can be very noisy. They originate in Central and South America and also include the Canarywing and Bebe.

The most common problems of the Brotogeris parakeets are bacterial infections (page 93), sarcoptic mange (page 148), chronic bacterial hepatitis (page 152), and psittacosis (page 69). Grey cheeks seem to have a high incidence of tuberculosis. Suspect it if your Brotogeris has weight loss, weakness, an enlarged abdomen, and diarrhea that does not respond to antibiotics.

They live ten to twenty years and weigh forty to fifty grams.

Conures

Conures are easy to tame and affectionate if acquired young. Not known for their talking ability, conures love to chew and are very noisy and active. They call Mexico and Central and South America home. Patagonian, Nanday, Sun, and Jenday are the most popular types. Nandays are screamers and are the least acceptable as pets. The saying goes, "If you want to give a gift to someone you don't like, give a Nanday conure."

Conures are suspected of carrying many different viruses, such as Pacheco's parrot disease and a herpes virus. Other common problems are bacterial infections and a bleeding disease.

They live ten to twenty-five years and weigh 80 to one hundred fifty grams.

Amazon Parrots

Amazons are not your warm, cuddly type of bird. They are talkative and very entertaining when sexually mature (five years old). Their behavior can be unpredictable and aggressive, especially during the mating season. Hand-raised babies make the best pets. The Amazons come in many varieties: yellow-naped, double yellow head, yellow-crowned, blue-front, orange-winged, green-cheeked, and Mealy. Their home base is Mexico and Central and South America.

Amazons' common problems are psittacosis, respiratory infections, vitamin A deficiency, and obesity. Cancer is common in older Amazons.

They live sixty to seventy years and weigh 400 to 900 grams.

African Greys

Young, hand-raised African greys can be very affectionate, sociable, and good talkers. Some may never utter a word, especially the wild-caught older birds, which are noisy and difficult to tame. Greys like to growl. This can be a sign of affection or a nasty, noisy habit when they are upset.

Some common African grey problems are feather picking (page 182), low blood calcium seizures (page 114), respiratory infections (bacterial or aspergillosis), and tapeworms.

African greys can live up to sixty to seventy years and weigh 400 to 500 grams.

Macaws

Macaws are large, intelligent, and playful. They require lots of room, attention, and chewing materials. They make good pets, but the wild-caught birds may be difficult to tame. Domestically bred, hand-raised macaws are wonderful. However, macaws should not be your first bird. They are only for the experienced bird owner.

Macaws call Mexico and Central and South America home.

The most common problems seen in macaws are macaw wasting disease (page 71); psittacosis (page 69); bacterial infections (page 93); behavioral problems—screaming, regurgitation, and aggression (page 184); feather cysts (page 148); and intestinal parasites (pages 65–69).

Macaws can live up to sixty or seventy years. They come in different sizes: scarlet, 1,000 grams; blue and gold, 1,000 grams; green-winged, 1,200 grams; and hyacinth, 1,400 grams.

Cockatoos

Cockatoos would like to be "surgically attached" to their owners. They are extremely affectionate and devoted. A large cage and a lot of attention, petting, and affection are needed. Chewing is one of their favorite activities, so you will need a good supply of wood and tree branches. The best bird is domestically bred and hand raised. Talk to your avian veterinarian about breeders.

They communicate with their crest and voice. Their beautiful crest goes up to signal excitement or aggression. Hissing is part of the cockatoos' "early warning system." They may become screamers if not given attention.

Most cockatoos produce abundant feather dust or powder, but this is normal. They are very picky eaters. This may lead to malnutrition and illness, so it is very important to work with your avian veterinarian on a well-balanced diet for your cockatoo.

They are from Australia, New Zealand, and the South Pacific islands.

The most common problems seen in cockatoos are psittacine beak and feather disease (page 70), bacterial infections (page 93), feather picking (page 182), blood parasites, and tapeworms.

The cockatoo's life span is twenty-five to fifty years, although some have lived over seventy years. Typical weights are as follows: greater sulfur-crested (800 grams), umbrella (600 grams), lesser sulfur-crested (500 grams), and rose-breasted (400 grams).

Mynahs

Mynahs are the finest talking birds. They will also mimic other everyday sounds—dogs barking, telephones ringing, or doors closing. It is best to get them before six months of age for taming and mimicry. They like a daily bath and a hide box for privacy.

Normally their droppings are loose and messy. The cage must be cleaned daily (see "Disinfectants," page 43). Mynahs need a very special diet (page 49).

Their original home is Southeast Asia, India, and the Philippines.

Mynah birds have a high incidence of liver diseases (iron storage disease, chronic active hepatitis, and cirrhosis). A liver test should be done at the "new-bird" exam and at the yearly physical exam. Bacterial infections are commonly seen, so cultures and sensitivities should be done routinely (page 81). Some my-nahs injure their corneas (keratitis) while being shipped.

Mynahs live ten to twenty-five years and weigh about 170 grams.

Toucans and Toucanettes

Toucans and their smaller relatives, the toucanettes, live in Mexico and Central and South America. Playful birds, they enjoy bathing and can be tamed, with time and patience. Their outstanding feature is a long, hollow, rainbow-colored beak. They do not talk or sing. Males and females look alike. They are very territorial and may kill strange birds or have domestic quarrels with their mates.

A special diet is required: mynah bird pellets, fresh fruit, and other selections from the "meat group"—cooked beef, chicken, tuna or other fish, and mature legumes (navy beans, kidney beans, or chick peas). In the wild, mice and small birds are eaten.

Daily cage cleaning is required since these birds are messy.

The common medical problems of toucans are liver diseases (similar to my-nahs), bacterial infections, and parasites (giardia and coccidia). Yearly liver tests, cultures, and parasite checks are recommended.

Toucans can live ten to twenty-five years and weigh from 300 grams (toucanettes) to 750 grams (Toco toucans).

Pigeons and Doves

When we think of pigeons, the city variety comes to mind. However, there are over 300 breeds of pigeons and four basic groups: (1) flying (rollers, tumblers, tipplers, skycutters—those that spin, somersault or do other "air-crobatics"); (2) racing homers (bred for their speed and homing ability); (3) show (the fancy and colorful birds bred to show—Jacobins and Pouters, for example); and (4) utilities (bred to eat—heavy birds with large breasts).

They mate for life but will take a new mate after a brief separation. The males are usually larger and more vocal, and they puff out their chests and strut. Pigeons are quiet, but they do like to coo.

There are commercial grain rations and pellet preparations for pigeons (and doves), which should be supplemented with some chicken layer pellet (19 to 20 percent protein). Include "pigeon health grit" and vitamins and minerals in their daily diet.

Pigeons are messy, so it is important to clean their cages and their food and water bowls *at least* once a day for control of diseases and parasites. Pigeons like to bathe.

The most common problems of pigeons and doves are parasites (intestinal worms, feather lice, red mites, pigeon fly); protozoal diseases; "canker" (trichomoniasis); coccidia (intestinal); blood parasites; viral diseases; pigeon pox; paramyvovirus; "eye colds" (mycoplasma—although it could also be ornithosis or bacterial infection); and salmonella (paratyphoid), causing loose droppings, weight loss, head-tilt or balancing problems, and "wing boils" (joint swellings).

Pigeons and doves can live ten to fifteen years. Their weight varies. American Giant Homers may be larger than chickens!

Lories and Lorikeets

These birds are very beautifully colored and affectionate. They have limited talking ability.

Their original home is Australia and the South Pacific islands.

A high-carbohydrate, nectarlike diet (commercially available) needs to be supplemented to keep these birds healthy. A good semiliquid diet recommended by Dr. Greg Harrison and Linda Harrison in their book, *Clinical Avian Medicine and Surgery,* is blended monkey biscuit, molasses, fresh apple, carrots, and water. This can be supplemented with spray millet, pollen, fruits, vegetables, mealworms, small seeds, and fresh branches.

The cage, bowls, and feeding solution must be changed *frequently* because the loose, messy droppings and the food with a high sugar content are good conditions for bacteria overgrowth.

Bathing in clean water is one of the lories' favorite activities. They must be housed with other birds of their own species with whom they are familiar, because they may kill other birds or newly introduced members of their own species.

Common medical problems among lories include bacteria and yeast (candida) infections from spoilage of their liquid diet and liver diseases.

Lories and lorikeets live ten to fifteen years and weigh 60 to 200 grams.

FINDING THE RIGHT BIRD FOR YOU

If you have decided that you can afford the time and money to own a bird, where can you go to select the new member of your family? Ask your veterinarian for a list of reputable breeders in the area. In addition, check the following publications:

AFA WATCHBIRD
American Federation of Aviculture
P. O. Box 1568
Redondo Beach, CA 90278
  (213) 372–2988

AMERICAN CAGE-BIRD MAGAZINE
One Glamore Ct.
Smithtown, NY 11787
  (516) 979–7962

BIRD TALK MAGAZINE
P. O. Box 6040
Mission Viejo, CA 92690
  (714) 240–6001

BIRD WORLD MAGAZINE
Box 70
N. Hollywood, CA 91603
  (818) 769–6111

A veterinary association with a special interest in bird care is the Association of Avian Veterinarians (P. O. Box 299, East Northport, NY 11731). A list of veterinarians by state may be obtained through A.A.V. Another useful association is the American Federation of Aviculture (P.O. Box 1568, Redondo Beach, CA 90278).

Pet shops that specialize in birds can be found in many cities. Try to avoid department stores or discount stores, where interest in and knowledge about birds are poor.

The larger parrots (Amazons, African greys, macaws, and cockatoos) are not easily bred. Currently, most of these birds are imported from their native areas, which creates a serious problem. It may often take up to *four months* for the parrots (Amazons, Senegals, African greys, macaws, and cockatoos) to arrive in the United States after capture. For example, the birds may be captured by using a net or a screaming decoy. Their wings are then clipped (many times poorly). If they are captured in Colombia, they may be stuffed in sacks and taken by dugout canoe to Panama, where payoffs are made. The birds may be kept in dirt-floor holding facilities and fed *only* sunflower seeds and water. Upon arrival in the United States, they must enter a quarantine facility near the area where they will be sold. Some birds may travel by way of Europe and then Canada before they reach the quarantine center, where they are kept in crowded quarters and given a poor diet.

Therefore that "new" bird that has "just" arrived from abroad has in fact been severely stressed by physical and mental trauma and malnutrition. These birds are very susceptible to viral, bacterial, yeast, and parasitic infections. Remember that these problems develop through the *legal* transportation of birds. Many birds are smuggled to avoid the added costs. Smuggled birds are even more traumatized and pose a health menace: Newcastle disease in poultry and psittacosis in humans.

As you can see, there is a lot to think about before you purchase one of the larger parrots. Don't be discouraged by this information—just make sure you give careful consideration to the place where you purchase the larger parrots and give your parrot the extra love and proper nutrition needed to overcome its ordeal.

Be sure that you purchase these parrots from a reputable person. Of course, the *best* place to purchase one of the larger parrots is from a *breeder.* Contact your veterinarian or one of the bird societies to see if the bird that you like is bred in captivity. If so, it is well worth the price to own a healthy and properly raised bird.

Select a bird that looks healthy. Watch out for trouble signs:

- Eye or nose discharges (staining of the feathers above the nostrils)
- Sneezing or coughing
- Shortness of breath
- Regurgitation or loose droppings
- Soiled vent
- Fluffing up
- Inactivity (it should not look sleepy and withdrawn)
- Bald spots where feathers should be
- Swelling or sores on the feet or toes (both feet should be able to grip the perch or your hand firmly)
- Protruding breastbone
- White crusts on the beak (which should be in good alignment)

Select a bird that seems temperamentally well balanced and shows interest in its surroundings and in your presence and voice.

BUYING YOUR BIRD

What should you expect—besides your new bird—at the time of payment? A reputable bird dealer will allow you to take a prospective pet to a veterinarian of your choice for examination within a few days of purchase. Your purchase should *always* be contingent upon the bird passing such an inspection, and you should be allowed to return the bird for a full refund if the animal is not in good health.

Purchase Papers

You should receive a *written bill of sale* stating

1. The aforementioned privilege of return
2. The date of purchase and any conditions of sale
3. The price paid
4. The bird's band number, if possible

5. The bird's birth date (if known) and a full description, including the bird's genus and species, sex, and color. Note: Frequently, the sex of parrots cannot be determined without an internal abdominal exam (called "scoping").

Instructions for Care

You should also be given written instructions on feeding and care. If the bird is imported, you should receive a copy of the quarantine certificate.

When you take your new bird home, be sure that it has plenty of time for rest and fresh food and water. Be gentle, patient, and quiet. After all, your bird has been brought to a strange home. Follow the written instructions for feeding and care until you see your veterinarian. If you have small children, be sure to instruct them carefully on how to handle the bird. You may want to be present the first few times your children are with the bird. Small birds are easily injured if they are dropped or squeezed by a child, and large parrots can inflict severe injuries to small children. If you have other birds, quarantine the new bird for thirty to sixty days. Your "old birds" should, of course, be already tested and free of all infectious diseases, and the new bird should be examined and tested by an avian veterinarian. Also read Aviculture Management, page 200, for some helpful tips.

RULES FOR BRINGING PET BIRDS INTO THE UNITED STATES
from the United States Department of Agriculture

What Is a Pet Bird?

A *pet bird* is defined as any bird—except for poultry—intended for the personal pleasure of its individual owner and not for resale. Poultry, even if kept as pets, are imported under separate rules and quarantined at USDA animal import centers. Birds classified as poultry include chickens, turkeys, pheasants, partridge, ducks, geese, swans, doves, peafowl, and similar avian species.

Importing a Pet Bird

Special Rules for Bringing a Pet Bird into the United States (from all countries but Canada)

- USDA quarantine
- Quarantine space reservation
- Fee in advance
- Foreign health certificate
- Final shipping arrangements
- Two-bird limit

If you're bringing your pet bird into the country, you must . . .

Quarantine your bird (or birds) for at least 30 days in a USDA-operated import facility at one of nine ports of entry. The bird, which must be caged when you bring it in, will be transferred to a special isolation cage at the import facility. Privately owned cages cannot be stored by USDA. Birds will be cared for by veterinarians and other personnel of USDA's Animal and Plant Health Inspection Service (APHIS).

Reserve quarantine space for the bird. A bird without a reservation will be accepted only if space is available. If none exists, this bird either will be refused entry or be transported—at your expense—to another entry port where there is space. In any case, the fee described below must be paid before the bird is placed in quarantine.

Pay USDA an advance fee of $80 to be applied to the cost of quarantine services and necessary tests and examinations. Currently, quarantine costs are expected to average $100 for one bird or $125 per isolation cage if more than one bird is put in a cage. These charges may change without notice. You may also have to pay private companies for brokerage and transportation services to move the bird from the port of entry to the USDA import facility.

Obtain a health certificate in the nation of the bird's origin. This is a certificate signed by a *national government* veterinarian stating that the bird has been examined, shows no evidence of communicable disease, and is being exported in accordance with the laws of that country. The certificate must be signed within 30 days of the time the birds arrive in the United States. If not in English, it must be translated at your cost. Please note that Form 17–23, referred to later, includes an acceptable health certificate form in English.

Arrange for shipping the bird to its final destination when it is released from quarantine. A list of brokers for each of the nine ports of entry may be requested from USDA port veterinarians at the time quarantine space is reserved. (See addresses to follow.) Most brokers offer transportation services from entry port to final destination.

Bring no more than two psittacine birds (parrots, parakeets, and other hookbills) per family into the United States during any one year. Larger groups of these birds are imported under separate rules for commercial shipments of birds.

Rules Effective since January 15, 1980

Why All the Rules?

Serious diseases of birds and poultry can be carried by pet birds entering this country. Parrots from South America are believed to have caused an outbreak of exotic Newcastle disease in southern California in 1971–74. Eradication cost $56 million and the destruction of 12 million birds, mostly laying hens. Import rules for personally owned pet birds were put into effect in 1972 and strengthened in 1980. These rules provide a better defense against the introduction of this highly contagious disease.

Ports of Entry for Personally Owned Pet Birds

Listed below are the nine ports of entry for personally owned pet birds. To reserve quarantine space for your bird, write to the port veterinarian at the city where you'll be arriving and request Form 17–23. Return the completed form, together with a certified check or money order for $80 made payable to USDA, to the same address. The balance of the fee will be due before the bird is released from quarantine.

Port Veterinarian
Animal and Plant Health Inspection Service
U. S. Department of Agriculture
(City, State, Zip Code)

Brownsville, TX 78520
El Paso, TX 79901
Honolulu, HI 96850

Laredo, TX 78040
Los Angeles, CA 90045
Miami, FL 33166
New York, NY 11430
Nogales, AZ 85621
San Ysidro, CA 92073

The Quarantine Period

During quarantine, pet birds will be kept in individually controlled isolation cages to prevent any infection from spreading. Psittacine or hook-billed birds will be identified with a leg band. They will be fed a medicated feed as required by the U.S. Public Health Service to prevent psittacosis, a flulike disease transmissible to humans. Food and water will be readily available to the birds. Young immature birds needing daily hand feeding cannot be accepted because removing them from the isolation cage for feeding would interrupt the thirty-day quarantine. During the quarantine, APHIS veterinarians will test the birds to make certain they are free of any communicable disease of poultry. Infected birds will be refused entry; at the owner's option they will either be returned to the country of origin (at the owner's expense) or humanely destroyed.

Special Exceptions

No government quarantine (and therefore no advance reservations or fees) and no foreign health certificate are required for:

U.S. birds taken out of the country for sixty days or less if special arrangements are made in advance. Before leaving the United States, you must get a health certificate for the bird from a veterinarian accredited by USDA and make certain it is identified with a tattoo or numbered leg band. The health certificate, with this identification on it, must be presented at the time of reentry. While out of the country, you must keep your pet bird separate from other birds. Remember that only two psittacine or hookbilled birds per family per year may enter the United States. Birds returning to the United States may come in through any one of the nine ports of entry listed earlier. There are also certain other specified ports of entry for these birds, depending upon the time of arrival and other factors. Contact APHIS officials for information on this before leaving the country.

Birds from Canada. Pet birds may enter the United States from Canada on your signed statement that they have been in your possession for at least ninety days, were kept separate from other birds during the period, and are healthy. As with other countries, only two psittacine birds per family per year may enter the United States from Canada. Birds must be inspected by an APHIS veterinarian at designated ports of entry for land, air, and ocean shipments. These ports are subject to change, so for current information, contact APHIS/USDA officials at the address listed in the section on U.S. agencies.

Pet birds from Canada are not quarantined because Canada's animal disease control and eradication programs and import rules are similar to those of the United States.

19

Other U.S. Agencies Involved with Bird Imports

In addition to the U.S. Public Health Service requirement mentioned earlier, U.S. Department of the Interior rules require an inspection by one of its officials to assure that an imported bird is not in the rare or endangered species category, is not an illegally imported migratory bird, and is not an agricultural pest or injurious to humans. Also, of course, the U.S. Customs Service maintains a constant alert for smuggled birds. For details from these agencies, contact:

Division of Law Enforcement
Fish and Wildlife Service
P. O. Box 28006
Washington, DC 20005

Bureau of Epidemiology
Quarantine Division
Center for Disease Control
U.S. Public Health Service
Atlanta, GA 30333

U.S. Customs Service
Department of the Treasury
Washington, DC 20229

For additional information on USDA/APHIS regulations, contact:
Import-Export Staff
Veterinary Services, APHIS
U.S. Department of Agriculture
Hyattsville, MD 20782

Two Serious Threats to Birds

Exotic Newcastle Disease

As a bird owner, you should know the symptoms of exotic Newcastle disease, the devastating disease of poultry and other birds mentioned elsewhere in this book. If your birds show signs of incoordination and breathing difficulties—or if there should be any unusual die-off among them—contact your local veterinarian or animal health official immediately. Place dead birds in plastic bags and refrigerate them for submittal to a diagnostic laboratory. Keep in mind that this disease is highly contagious, and you should isolate any newly purchased birds for at least thirty days. Although exotic Newcastle disease is not a general health hazard, it can cause minor eye infection in humans directly exposed to infected birds.

Smuggling

If you're tempted to buy a bird you suspect may have been smuggled into the United States . . . *don't!* Smuggled birds are a persistent threat to the health of pet birds and poultry flocks in this country. Indications are that many recent outbreaks of exotic Newcastle disease were caused by birds entering the United States illegally. If you have information about the possibility of smuggled birds, report it to any U.S. Customs office or call APHIS at Hyattsville, Maryland (301) 436–8061.

2

The Owner's Home Physical Exam

YOUR BIRD'S BODY AND HOW IT WORKS

The next day in the back yard, I use the old saw horses and a four-by-four as a perch to practice with. I put my perch up three feet and take a running jump flapping my arms. I realize how much spring those baby birds have in their legs already. If the spring in the legs develops in comparative strength the same as the wings, a grown bird must be able to hop, even without wings, almost as well as a frog. It would be interesting to see how a bird growing up without wings would behave. I don't mean a penguin or something that gave up flying to be able to swim, but a bird who naturally would fly but doesn't have wings.

That night my arms are deadly sore from flapping, but I keep it up. If those little birds can do it, I can, too. I get so I can jump up on the perch and stay there. My main problem is the same one they have, that is, stopping my forward motion and not going over the other side of the perch. I flap my arms to keep myself balanced.

What I need is a tail. I could put some cloth sewn to my trousers between my legs, but that wouldn't help. The tail has to be completely independent of the legs and controllable. Already those babies can tilt their tail up and down and spread the feathers . . . I'm still keeping up with them but already I can see that I don't have a chance without mechanical help. The one thing I know is I don't want a motor or anything like that. If I can't fly on my own power, then I don't want it.

. . . I practice out in the yard doing these things for about an hour every night and I flap a half hour in the morning and another half hour before I go to bed at night. I close my eyes when I flap and try to imagine I'm flying. I'm trying to get the rhythm of it across my shoulders. If I can just loosen the scapula and open up the acromeon process at the shoulder some and then develop the trapezius, deltoid, and triceps muscles, I could build up a lot of flapping power.

I practice jumping with each flap so I'll get a smooth movement. . . . I try to twist my shoulders in circles, grabbing air under my armpits. That's the way birds seem to do it. I'm flapping with weights in my hands now. My shoulders and neck are beginning to get bumpy. If I'm not careful, I'll walk around with my head sticking out in front of me.

So says Birdy, the main character in William Wharton's wonderfully entertaining novel *Birdy* (Alfred A. Knopf, 1978).

Birdy dreamed of flying on his own power and thinking like a bird. He felt that this was the ultimate experience and what we call *to be free.* Of course, Birdy or

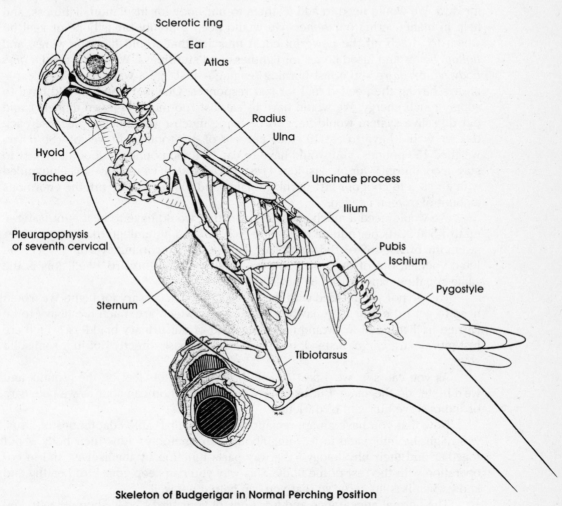

Skeleton of Budgerigar in Normal Perching Position

From *Diseases of Cage and Aviary Birds,* 2nd edition, by Margaret L. Petrak, Copyright 1982 Lea and Febiger Publishing Company. Used by permission.

any other human would need a considerable overhaul in order to become the ultimate "flying machine." We would need huge *chest muscles* (that would put Arnold Schwarzenegger to shame) to rapidly flap the *wings* that would lift and propel us forward. We would need to add feathers to our body for insulation, lightness, and help in maneuvering our *bones.* We would need a pointy breastbone or keel on which to attach all the powerful chest muscles that would flap our wings, and *hollow bones* and fused bones for lightness and sturdiness. We would need a *high body temperature* and a fast-burning "engine"—just like a warmed-up race car—always having the needed fuel for fast responses. Our fuel (food) would have to supply much energy. We would have to eat fast (no more sit-down dinners), and our digestive system would have to be made much more efficient because each day we would have to eat 10 to 25 percent of our total body weight. (So if you weighed 150 pounds, you would have to eat 15 to 40 pounds of food daily just to stay in condition!) Our old-fashioned *respiratory system* would have to be upgraded with air sacs to cool our fast-burning engine and to provide us with the enormous amount of oxygen needed.

We would need a much stronger heart that would have to beat a lot faster—up to 1,500 beats per minute if we were to become a hummingbird. Have you ever swum the breaststroke? Did your heart feel like it was working overtime when you lifted yourself out of the water and propelled yourself forward? Well, this is the same situation experienced by birds in flight.

We are not yet finished with the modifications necessary for flight. We would need to get rid of our large jawbones and teeth, which are much too heavy to be carried in flight, and we would need to get rid of our urinary bladders, which are just more extra cargo. Instead, our wastes would pass directly out in a semisolid state.

As you can see, we'd best advise Birdy to keep his feet on the ground, and we'd better do the same. But like Birdy, our imagination can soar as we take care of and observe our wild bird friends.

Now that you have an appreciation for the remarkable adaptations of birds, you might be interested in learning about their anatomy—how their body is put together and their physiology—the way parts function by themselves and in cooperation with the rest of the body. This way you can keep your bird healthy and know when it is ill, *early,* so that you can help it get well.

The normal appearance and functions of your bird's body should be studied so that by using the Decision Charts included here and by doing a simple physical exam, you will be better prepared to know when to treat your bird at home and when to take it to your veterinarian.

It's a good idea to examine healthy birds about once every six months. If your bird doesn't look well, it's advisable to run through the exam again.

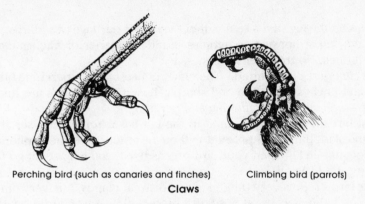

Perching bird (such as canaries and finches)   Climbing bird (parrots)
Claws

FEATHERS AND SKIN

The skin of birds has many remarkable modifications—feathers, scales, claws, and the preen gland.

Feathers protect the body and are important for flying. They protect wild birds from rain, the sun's rays, and skin injury. All birds can fluff and ruffle their feathers to form the air pockets that insulate them against chills or the cold. *Watch for a fluffed, ruffled appearance—it may be an early sign of illness.* Feathers also have other functions: they can signal sexual or aggressive displays, and they can be used as nest material. For example, canaries may pick their own feathers or those of their nestlings to form that architectural wonder—the nest.

There are three main types of feathers: *contour, down,* and *filioplume.* The *contour* feathers form the main plumage of the wings, tail, and body, which gives a bird its shape or contour. Each feather has a long stalk or vane with many interlocking barbs. *Filioplumes* are hairlike feathers that have a thin stalk and a fluffy tuft at the tip. *Down* feathers form the main plumage on nestlings and are found under the contour feathers in adults. Down supplies insulation par excellence by trapping air near the bird's body. Such feathers have a short shaft and many non-interlocking barbs.

The flight feathers on the wing are named according to their location. The primaries are the ones that are attached to what would be equivalent to our hand area; the secondaries are attached to the "forearm" area. Gently unfold the wing and you will see all the flight feathers.

Birds would not be able to fly or insulate themselves if old, worn-out feathers were not replaced. This process is called *molting,* and it can be compared with the shedding of the hair of humans, dogs, or cats.

Be aware of your bird's normal, healthy feather condition. *Failure to lose old, worn-out, frayed feathers or to replace areas with new feathers could be a sign of illness.* Look for other coexisting signs of illness.

Scales on the legs are a remnant of the reptile heritage of all birds. They serve as protective leg armor and sometimes in older canaries or finches can get quite pointy and thick. No treatment is necessary.

The *claws* are "form-fitted." The claws of passerines—perching birds such as canaries and finches—are thin and sharp. Those of psittacines are thick, curved, and sharp—well suited for climbing and perching.

Most birds have a *preen gland* in the tail base. You cannot see it since it is beneath the skin, but its oil product is thought to lubricate the feathers and to be a source of vitamin D. When your bird preens itself, you may see it go to its "back pocket" to get a little oil.

Your bird's *skin* is very thin and has no sweat glands. It is very different from our skin—probably because it is so well protected by a wonderful "feather coat."

THE MUSCULOSKELETAL SYSTEM

Without the support and protection of bones, your bird would collapse into a pile of feathers. Bird bones have fascinating modifications. Many have air sacs or are hollow (lightness for flight). The breastbone is keel-shaped (so that the large, powerful flight muscles will have adequate room for attachment), and other bones are fused or eliminated (to provide less weight and a more rigid flying and landing structure). Skull bones and some of the spinal bones are fused. Birds have a reduction of fingers and wrist bones: the first and fifth "fingers" are not present and the others are partially fused. Many leg bones are fused. Canaries and finches (passerines or perching birds) have three toe bones pointing forward and one backward. The psittacines, who are vigorous climbers, have two toes forward and two backward for good grasping power. Birds would have a tough time getting off the ground if they had a thick jawbone like ours; thus, the jawbone is lighter and reduced in size. The neck bones are so modified that birds can turn their heads completely around to preen or to spot a friend or foe. The two essential minerals—calcium and phosphorus—are largely stored in, as well as inventoried and distributed by, the bones. Without calcium, a bird's heart could not beat, the wings could not flap, and the nerves could not conduct messages. Without adequate amounts of these minerals, breeding birds will produce thin-shelled eggs or become egg-bound. Old red and white blood cells must be replaced, so they are constantly being manufactured by the spongy bone marrow and sent out into the bloodstream.

Home Physical Exam

- Observe how your bird uses its limbs for climbing and perching. Are both legs used equally? Are both wings held the same way? Are there any joint swellings? Are there any deformities of the wings, legs, or toes?

- To examine the individual areas of your bird's skeletal system, you may find it helpful to locate your own corresponding bones and joints first.

MUSCLES

After receiving messages from the nerves, the muscles flap the wing bones, move the legs, or flick the tail. These are the skeletal muscles that your bird consciously moves. There are over 150 pairs of muscles that help your bird flap, flick, fly, peck, sing, or talk. Two special types of muscles work day and night involuntarily. The heart (cardiac) muscle contracts with less than a one-quarter second rest between beats throughout a bird's life. Smooth muscle tissue, which moves food along the digestive tract, is also primarily involuntary.

Home Physical Exam

- Your main focus will be the size of the breast (pectoral) and thigh muscles.
- The keel-shaped breastbone or sternum houses the huge, powerful *pectoral* muscles that flap the wings. If a bird is losing weight, the muscles on the breast may become smaller, and the pointed keel will seem more prominent. The thigh muscles may also become smaller if weight is lost.

EYES

Birds have highly developed eyesight. The eyeball is very large, making it possible to see sharper images, especially when flying at great height and speed. In fact, if we had similarly powerful eyes, they would take up about half of our head. Most of the eyeball is protected and hidden from view by specialized "curtains"—the upper and lower eyelids. These are the first things you will see when examining your bird's eyes. Eyelashes are located on the edges of both lids. Examine the eyelids; they should be smooth and sharp. A smooth, pink tissue called the *conjunctiva* can be seen covering the inner surface of the lids and continuing on the eyeball. The conjunctiva helps lubricate the eyeball and protect it from infection. The space between the eyelid conjunctiva and the eyeball conjunctiva is the *conjunctival sac.* If the conjunctiva is red and swollen or if there is a discharge, an inflammation of the tissue is present.

Birds (like snakes, dogs, cats, and other animals) have a structure called the *third eyelid,* or *nictitating membrane,* which contributes to tear formation and distribution as it sweeps across the eyeball from the inner to the outer corner of the eye. Light pink in color, the third eyelid is located at the inner corner of the eye.

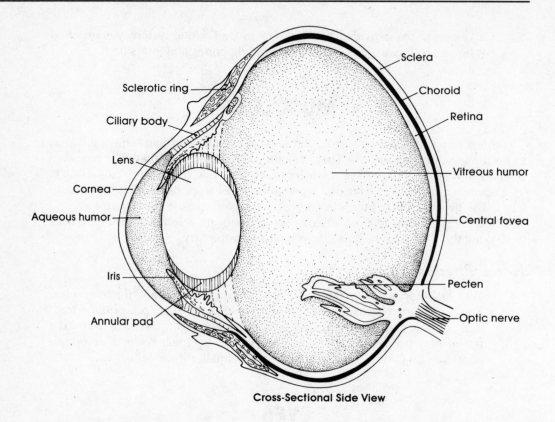

Sclerotic ring

Ciliary body

Lens

Cornea

Aqueous humor

Iris

Annular pad

Sclera

Choroid

Retina

Vitreous humor

Central fovea

Pecten

Optic nerve

Cross-Sectional Side View

The *cornea* is the clear "front window" of the eye that bends the incoming light rays. The cornea can lose its clarity if it becomes inflamed or injured.

The *sclera* is the fibrous coat that gives the eyeball its spherical shape and dull white color. (This is often called the "white" of the eye.)

The *iris* controls the amount of light entering the back of the eye and gives the eye its color. The black hole in the center of the iris is the *pupil*. It *dilates* in dim light to let more light enter and *constricts* in bright light. Shining a bright light in one eye should constrict both pupils, which should be the same shape and size.

Light rays enter the eye's fluid-filled *anterior chamber,* pass through the pupil, and are further bent by the lens as they continue their journey through the *vitreous body,* a transparent jellylike substance that keeps the eyeball firm. The light rays finally hit the "heart" of the eye—the *retina,* which is located at the back of the eye. The retina is a membrane having more than 100 million light-sensitive cells called rods and cones. These cells set off a flurry of electrochemical activity that transmits an image to the brain by way of the optic nerve in about two-thousandths of a second.

The retina has a pigmented, highly vascular fold of tissue, called the *pecten,* which projects into the vitreous. It is thought to provide the retina with oxygen and nutrition, and it removes waste products.

Cataracts—white opacities in the lens that block the light's passage through the eye—are sometimes seen in older birds.

Tears cover the eye with each blink. They keep the eyes moist and help protect them from foreign objects, bacteria, and viruses. Tears are formed by the *secretion* of glands located around the inner lids and behind the third eyelid. They drain from the eye through a canal system that runs from the *medial canthus* (inner corner) of the eye to the nostrils. (This is why your nose runs when you cry.)

Home Physical Exam

- The *eyelids* should be smooth and sharp, not be swollen or crusty.
- There should be no *eye discharge* and no closing of the eye in pain (*blepharospasm*).
- The *conjunctiva,* or eye lining, should be smooth and pink.
- The eye should not bulge from its socket—common in parrots with abscesses around the eye and in the nasal sinus.
- The *cornea* should be clear.
- The *pupils* should be the same size and shape and respond to light equally. There should be no white opacity (*cataract*) in the pupil.

EARS

The ears are located slightly behind and below the eye. Of course, no earlobes are present. (They would weigh too much! Furthermore, birds must conserve heat to maintain their high body temperature. A lot of heat is lost from *our* ear lobes.)

The small ear canal can be seen if you part the feathers. The *eardrum* is at the end of the canal. Sound waves travel down the canal and beat against the eardrum—like a stick beating a drum. The vibrations are amplified in the *middle ear* by a small, rodlike bone called the *columella,* which passes the sound on to the inner ear's fluid-filled *cochlea* via the *oval window* (a vibrating membrane). The waves produced in the cochlea are converted to electrical messages that travel to your bird's brain via the *auditory nerve.*

Above the cochlea are three small fluid-filled *semicircular canals.* These loops of tubing contribute to your bird's remarkable sense of balance. For example, in a swoop down from one perch to another, fluid in one of the canals is displaced. Hair cells in the canals detect the change and immediately keep the brain informed so that the muscles can be ordered to tighten or loosen for a perfect, balanced landing.

Home Physical Exam

- Locate the ear behind and below the eye.
- Check for any discharges, swelling, cuts or wounds.
- Check your bird's balance. A wobbly bird may have an inflamed or traumatized balancing mechanism.
  (*Note:* Ear problems are uncommon in birds.)

THE CIRCULATORY SYSTEM

The hardest worker in your bird's body is the heart. It is a four-chambered model (just like the human heart) that actually consists of two pumps. The right side of the heart receives the blue blood (depleted of oxygen) that has already dropped off its cargo of oxygen and nutrients and has returned with waste products, such as carbon dioxide, by way of the veins. This blue blood is pumped through the lungs and air sacs to receive fresh oxygen and to remove the carbon dioxide. The blood then returns to the left side of the heart and is pumped out through the arteries to the trillions of cells in your bird's body.

If you were to tap your finger on a table 200 to 1,300 times per minute, your finger would get very tired. Yet that is the heart rate, day and night, in all birds. Because of their high rate of metabolism, birds need large quantities of oxygen quickly—thus their very high heart rate. The hummingbird's heart beats about 1,300 times per minute, which is over 20 times per second.

Home Physical Exam

- You can estimate your bird's heart rate by placing your fingers or your ear (watch your eyes) against your bird's chest or by using a stethoscope, which can be purchased at a medical supply store. The normal heart rate is so fast that it is a difficult counting job even for your veterinarian. Count the number of beats in 15 seconds. Multiply the number by 4. For example: 70 beats in 15 seconds = 70 × 4 = 280 beats per minute.

Heart rate (beats per minute)

Canary	500–800
Finches	500–800
Budgerigars	300–500
Small parrots	250–350
Macaws	200
Cockatoos	200

• Older parrots are prone to blockages of the neck arteries (stroke) and heart disease. Some signs may be sudden paralysis or breathing difficulties.

THE LYMPHATIC SYSTEM

The *lymphatic system* aids the heart and blood vessels. It filters out invaders and transports to the bloodstream, in a watery substance called *lymph,* the antibodies and lymphocytes produced in lymph follicles. There are no lymph nodes such as tonsils in birds.

THE RESPIRATORY SYSTEM

Birds, like people, need to gather oxygen from the air and to expel carbon dioxide (a waste product of metabolism). But unlike humans or any other animal, birds need large amounts of oxygen-rich air rapidly and constantly for their high metabolic rate and for flying. Fortunately, they are blessed with a most efficient respiratory system. The nostrils, mouth, larynx, trachea, syrinx, bronchi, lungs, air sacs, ribs, and chest muscles make it all possible.

Air is inhaled through two *nostrils* located at the base of the beak. In birds such as budgerigars, a fleshy structure called the *cere* houses the nostrils. The air is warmed and moistened as it passes through the nasal cavity to the *glottis,* the slitlike but expandable opening in the back of the throat. The oxygen-rich air continues its rapid journey through the *larynx* and the *trachea,* the long breathing tube in the neck (windpipe). The larynx is our voice box, but the bird's larynx is not used for voice or song. That job is handled by the *syrinx,* which is located in the chest where the trachea divides into two smaller breathing tubes called the *bronchi.* The oxygen-rich air is warmed and filtered of dust, bacteria, and viruses before it reaches its final destinations, the *lungs* and *air sacs*—the "heart" of this most remarkable breathing system. Fresh oxygen-rich air is thought to be constantly available thanks to the thin-walled, balloonlike storage areas called *air sacs,* which pass the air through the smaller interconnecting bronchi of the lungs where capillaries, small microscopic vessels, serve as the unloading dock for oxygen and the loading dock for the soon-to-be-exhaled waste product, carbon dioxide. The air sacs are also important in cooling your bird's body as water is evaporated (and heat is lost). Since these "baggage compartments" are filled with air, they make your bird extremely light for flight.

The lungs don't have any muscles. They expand only when the chest expands. The *diaphragm* (a muscular divider between the chest and abdomen) is not com-

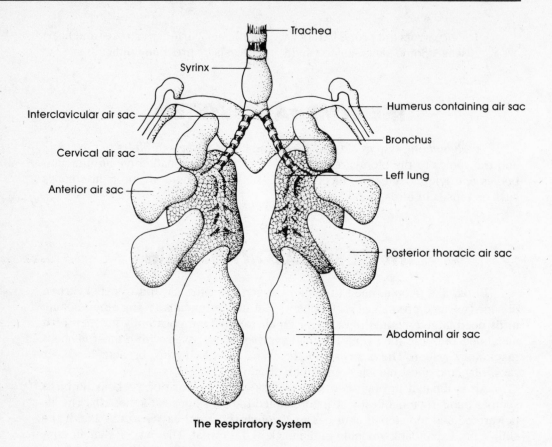

Trachea

Syrinx

Humerus containing air sac

Interclavicular air sac

Bronchus

Cervical air sac

Left lung

Anterior air sac

Posterior thoracic air sac

Abdominal air sac

The Respiratory System

plete in the bird and does not seem to play an important role in respiration, as it does in dogs, cats, and humans.

Small birds such as finches, canaries, and budgerigars have a normal resting breathing rate of about 100 breaths per minute. Large parrots such as macaws and cockatoos take about 30 to 40 breaths per minute.

Home Physical Exam

- Check your bird's *breathing rate.* It should be about 30 breaths per minute (larger parrots) to 100 per minute (smaller birds) in a normal resting state when not excited or in a hot environment.
- After exercise, your bird's breathing rate should return to normal within one or two minutes.
- Your bird should breathe in and out with no exertion.
- Check the *nostrils.* There should be no swelling around them and no dis-

charge. Sometimes the feathers around the nostrils will be stained brown from a nasal discharge.

- Check for *sneezing*. Listen closely. A bird's "achoo" is barely heard—but it may be the beginning of a serious respiratory problem.
- We often get hoarse when we get a cold. So do birds. So if your bird speaks hoarsely or sings with a different sound, the *syrinx* (voice box) may be inflamed.
- Birds *cough* but not as dramatically as we do. You may just hear a faint "clicking" sound. Keep your ears open for this potentially serious sign.

THE DIGESTIVE SYSTEM

A bird's digestive system is tailor-made to its special requirements, with a "pouch" (the crop) for storing food while on the go and a system that rapidly digests food and delivers it to the bloodstream.

A discussion of your bird's digestive system should start with its teeth. Teeth? Fossils indicate that about 130 million years ago birds such as archaeopteryx had teeth and a huge, heavy jaw to go with them. Evolution was kind to birds. Teeth were replaced by beaks, which were well suited to the type of food eaten and made the bird less top heavy.

Beaks and *tongues* are modified according to the bird's diet and habits. For example, the huge, curved beak and thick tongue of the parrot are well suited for climbing and for cracking nuts and large seeds and removing the kernel from the shell, whereas the thin, curved beak of the hummingbird is designed for sucking nectar.

The beak grows constantly and must be worn down by use—cracking seeds, rubbing on a perch or cuttlebone, or climbing.

The food passes from the mouth to the *esophagus*. This muscular tube transports the food by waves, which are called *peristalsis,* to the *crop*—a pouchlike storage area located at the bottom of the neck. It can be seen, especially if it contains seed, when you separate the feathers at the neck base.

The food next passes into the stomach—the most active performer in your bird's digestive system—which has two parts. A small tubelike *proventriculus,* or "glandular stomach," secretes digestive juices that help break down the food. In the budgerigar, this organ can produce "crop milk," a very nutritious mixture fed to nestlings. The proventriculus joins the large "muscular stomach" known as the *ventriculus,* or *gizzard.*

Seed eaters and nut eaters have particularly muscular gizzards that grind up food with the help of grit—gravel, sand, or pebbles. In fact in 1783, Spallanzani found that the powerful gizzard of the turkey could grind twelve steel needles to pieces in thirty-six hours.

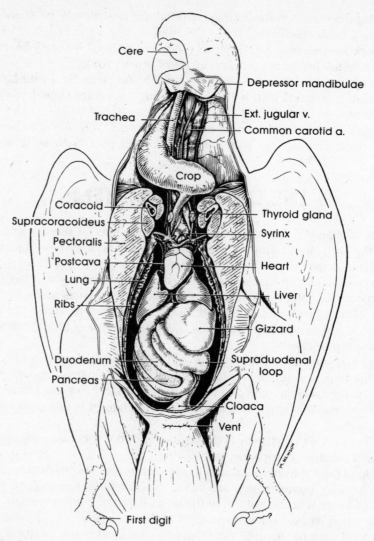

The Digestive Tract

From *Diseases of Cage and Aviary Birds,* 2nd edition, by Margaret L. Petrak. Copyright 1982 by Lea and Febiger Publishing Company. Used by permission.

After leaving the gizzard, the food enters the small intestine, where it is mixed with bile from the *liver* and enzymes from the *pancreas*.

The liver has two equal lobes, but it cannot be palpated or seen in the normal bird since it nestles next to the heart under the rib cage. The liver produces the proteins that provide strength for your bird's enormous flight muscles, it manufactures the clotting agents that stop the bleeding of a cut, and it plays an important role in fat and sugar metabolism. In addition, the liver is the "great detoxifier"—purifying toxins and drugs in your bird's system—and it recycles red blood cells; some red blood cells are used to make *bile,* the green digestive juice stored in the *gall bladder.* (By the way, budgerigars, pigeons, and some members of the parrot family don't have a gallbladder.) The bile helps break down large fat molecules.

In birds, the *pancreas* is located near the upper small intestine (the *duodenum*). The first function of this organ is to neutralize the acids in the mixture that the stomach passes on to the intestines. These acids are no laughing matter; they could inflict serious damage to the intestines if not neutralized. Your bird's pancreas also produces an impressive array of enzymes that are important in sugar, fat, and protein digestion. The pancreas is best known, however, for its manufacture of *insulin,* which ensures that all your bird's cells get large quantities of *glucose,* a simple sugar, for their enormous energy needs.

All nutrients are absorbed in the small intestine, which passes them to the bloodstream and lymphatic systems. Some birds have a *cecum,* or "appendix," that helps digest grains and fibers. It is not present in budgerigars and some parrots. The last stop is the *large intestine,* where water is extracted for your bird's use and the *feces* become firmer.

All indigestible material has to leave the body by way of the *cloaca*—the single opening for eliminating waste products from the digestive and urinary systems. If your bird is a seed-eater, its normal droppings should be targetlike in shape and consist of a black or dark green firm part (feces) and softer white part (urine). A bird should have between twenty-five and fifty eliminations per day. (You can see the odds are high that you may be hit by "good luck" on occasion by a bird flying overhead.) The majority of the droppings should be of the target variety, and a few shapeless watery droppings should not be of any concern unless other signs of illness are present. The droppings of fruit eaters and mynahs are normally loose.

The bird's digestive system is extremely efficient. Fruit eaters will digest and eliminate berries within thirty minutes, and seed and nut eaters will digest their food in only three hours.

Home Physical Exam

- The *beak* should not be overgrown.
- There should be no white crusts, discharges, or growths around the beak or in the mouth.
- There should be no odor in the *mouth.* (Smell it, but watch your nose!)
- Your bird should not have any difficulty swallowing, picking up food, or husking seeds.
- Some *regurgitation* may be normal.

- At the bottom of the neck, the crop may be seen or felt when filled with seed, but it should not be saclike (*pendulous crop*), flopping over the breast area.
- Your bird should not strain when defecating.
- Your bird should have twenty-five to fifty formed, target-shaped droppings per day and no bleeding.
- Count the droppings when you clean the cage each day. Fewer droppings may mean that your bird is not eating as much as usual, which may be the earliest sign of illness.
- Gently palpate the abdomen. The only organs that can be felt in a normal bird are the muscular gizzard and the intestines. All the other organs lie very deep or under the ribs and breastbone.

THE UROGENITAL SYSTEM

Your bird's kidneys are its main waste disposal plant. The paired kidneys clean and filter the blood continuously as it passes through them. They regulate the amount of salt, potassium, and water that is needed in the body. The excess is passed on with the waste products of metabolism through two tiny tubes called *ureters*. Birds have no storage tank like our bladder. (All that excess water would make flying a problem.) The ureters enter the *cloaca,* where the urine (the firm white part) is excreted, usually mixed with your bird's black or dark green feces, in the characteristic targetlike shape.

Home Physical Exam

- *Loose droppings* may indicate a urinary problem.
- The normal kidneys lie very deep in the abdomen and cannot be felt unless they become enlarged (which is not uncommon if there are kidney tumors, especially in budgerigars).

THE REPRODUCTIVE SYSTEM

Now for the "birds and bees." The sperm factories of the male bird are the paired, bean-shaped *testes*. Located at the front end of the kidneys, the testes produce the sex hormones that play an important role in the bright colors and cheerful courtship songs of many birds. The sperm (hundreds of millions of them) pass down the coiled thin-tubed vas deferens to the cloaca. There are many variations on these basic structures in different birds. The left testis enlarges tremendously

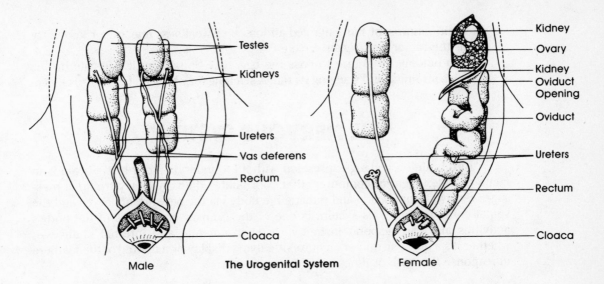

Male	Female

The Urogenital System

during breeding in some; in others there is an area at the back end of the vas deferens for sperm storage. Mating in birds is usually accomplished by the male mounting the back of the female. The cloacas are placed together, and the sperm is transferred to the female. In such birds as ducks and chickens the male has a penislike sex organ.

Female birds have one active sex gland, the left *ovary*. The right ovary usually is small and nonfunctional. The ovary, which is located at the front end of the kidney, will produce eggs ("egg yolks") during the breeding season. The eggs enter the funnel-shaped *infundibulum*—the entrance of the long-tubed *oviduct*. The sperm swim up and meet the egg in the upper oviduct. As it passes down the oviduct, the albumen, or "white of the egg," is added. The "shell gland" of the large muscular uterus provides the familiar shell to the "egg." If the egg shells are to be spotted, the pigment is "painted on" by glands in the uterus. The egg yolk and white provide the self-contained nutrition needed for healthy development of the baby-bird-to-be.

As with the testes, sex hormones are produced in the ovary that determine mating behavior, feathers, and coloring during the breeding season.

Home Physical Exam

- In the mature budgerigar, the *cere* is blue in the male and pink or brown in the female.
- Some birds, especially budgerigars, can develop tumors of the sex organs that may often be malignant. A common sign may be the color of a male's cere changing from blue to brown. (*Note:* This does not necessarily mean a

tumor is present.) An enlarged abdomen or weakness may occur in one leg as the tumor gets bigger.
- Egg binding, or failure to pass the egg, may be present if a female bird is seen straining and wagging its tail. A swelling may be seen below the cloaca.

THE NERVOUS SYSTEM

"Bird brain" is a slang expression without foundation. Your bird's brain is in fact a complex "central computer" that coordinates the very heavy traffic of messages received from inside and outside the body via the network of nerves and the spinal cord. The nervous system is one of the primary controllers of the body's activities and can respond instantly to environmental and internal changes— whether it's a quick swoop or an acrobatic flying display or a fluffing of the feathers in response to a chill or illness.

Home Physical Exam

- Sleepiness, change of personality, seizures, circling or paralysis may indicate a nervous system disorder.

THE ENDOCRINE SYSTEM

There are small chemical factories tucked away in obscure corners of your bird's body. These are called the *endocrine glands,* whose specialty products are hormones (from the Greek word meaning "to arouse activity"). Hormones regulate chemical reactions. The endocrine system primarily regulates processes of long duration, such as growth and reproduction.

Malfunctions of endocrine glands such as *diabetes* and *hypothyroidism* are seen in birds—especially budgerigars and cockatiels.

Home Physical Exam

- Increased water intake, watery droppings, and weight loss may be a sign of diabetes.
- Some feather disorders and weight gain may be related to an underactive thyroid gland.
- A lack of male hormones may cause a canary to stop singing.

Keeping Your Bird Happy & Healthy

HOME

A house becomes a *home* when each occupant (whether human, bird, dog, or cat) finds it to be a secure place with mostly happy moments.

A proper home is important for your bird's physical and mental health. Birds, like humans, need a cozy home, social contact, and a place that they can "escape to" for peace, quiet, and "thinking." If this is not provided, your bird may become physically ill from stress or may develop mental problems that lead to feather picking, constant squawking, toe chewing, or constant head motions (especially in the larger parrots) that take the form of figure eights, constant bowing, or side-to-side head movements.

Birds are usually housed in a cage or aviary. An aviary consists of a sheltered indoor or outdoor space and a flight area. Most people think that a little bird needs a little space. Well, that's inhumane. If you have room for an aviary in a spare room, even for your finches or canaries, by all means build it. They'll be as "happy as larks." Good books for aviary construction and just about any other construction project for your birds are *How to Build Everything You Need for Your Birds* by Don La Rosa, and *Building an Aviary* by Carl Strombergs.

A bird's living area must meet several requirements. It must be

- A roomy home
- A sturdy home
- Without drafts and away from gas fumes or other odors
- Easy to clean and maintain
- A place to eat and drink
- A "private room" to get away from it all or to sleep
- An exercise area
- A stable environment without changes in routine
- A place allowing social contact

A Roomy Home

In general, your birds should be able to stretch out their wings without touching the sides, and they should be able to fly comfortably from perch to perch. The larger the cage, the happier your birds will be. When on the perch, their heads should not touch the cage top, nor should their tail feathers touch the sides or the floor.

A Sturdy Home

The all-metal cages are best—and a "must" for all parrots, since they love to climb and chew on the cage. If you use a stand, be sure it cannot be tipped over easily. Cages with horizontal bars are great for climbers.

Larger parrots such as macaws and cockatoos need a cage made of strong wire mesh or wrought iron because of their powerful beaks. These large parrots do better if they are not caged most of the time. This will be explained later.

Without Drafts and Away from Gas Fumes and Other Odors

Drafts and sudden changes in temperature can chill your bird. Gas fumes or other odors (even some cooking odors) can cause respiratory or intestinal problems. Offensive odors such as tar from a nearby construction site can produce sickness and anxiety (feather plucking, head bowing, figure-eights, or side-to-side head movements). Do not use cookware or drip pans with Teflon or Silverstone. The fumes emitted can kill your bird. See "Convulsions and Seizures," page 114, and "Inhaled Poisons," page 130.

Easy to Clean and Maintain

Cage floors should be a wire mesh. The droppings will pass through to an easily cleaned, removable tray. Metal cages are easy to wash down with soap, water, and disinfectant. Use paper to line the bottoms. Do not use gravel paper, wood shavings, kitty litter, or corn cobs. Gravel paper irritates the feet. Wood shavings and kitty litter can be eaten and cause GI tract blockage. Corn cob can cause blockage and is a source of a dangerous fungus of the respiratory tract, aspergillus.

A Place to Eat and Drink

The food and water dishes should be plastic, ceramic, or stainless steel (for parrots)—and washed on a daily basis.

A "Private Room" to Get Away from It All

Birds like to have some privacy. A wooden breeding box (even for nonbreeders) attached to the cage is a welcome delight to most birds. The larger parrots enjoy wooden barrels with a round entrance hole on the side. These structures have to be kept clean and dry.

An Exercise Area

See the section on aerobics and exercise in this chapter.

A Stable Environment

Birds like stability. Routines—feeding, watering, and cage cleaning—should be done at the *same time* every day. So should training. Birds need twelve hours of darkness for sleeping. Any change in routine can cause stress and physical illness or behavior problems such as feather plucking or toe chewing. The same goes for new family members, or new sounds or odors in your bird's surroundings. If your bird seems to be having a medical problem (loose droppings, for example) or behavior problem, examine the changes that have occurred at about the same time in your bird's routine or environment.

A Place Allowing Social Contact

Birds are social animals. Canaries and finches are more social with their own kind than with humans, but many bird owners have tamed them to a point where they seek out human contact.

Parrot family members, such as budgerigars, cockatiels, lovebirds, African greys, amazons, macaws, and cockatoos, need affection and thrive on company—other birds, humans, and sometimes even dogs. Some parrots love to hitch a ride on the family dog's back. If you do not have a companion for your parrot or don't have the time to spend with your bird, don't get a member of the parrot family.

SUNLIGHT AND ARTIFICIAL LIGHT

Birds need sunlight or artificial light. On warm days, you and your bird can profit from real sunlight. The ultraviolet rays are important for activating vitamin D production and calcium absorption and for stimulating reproduction. Make sure that your bird is supervised in a *secure* cage when you are outside (sit with him or her); otherwise, a wandering cat could make a meal of your bird. Some shade should also be provided.

Artificial light can provide the complete spectrum of important light. Vita-lite is available from your avian veterinarian and from plant, hardware, or pet stores.

DISINFECTANTS

Rotting food and feces are good sources of bacteria, fungus and virus "gardens"—potential threats to your bird's health.

The food and water bowls should be cleaned and disinfected daily. The cage needs a "housecleaning" weekly. Scrub with soap and hot water. It is important to remove all the dirt and debris so that the disinfectant can kill all the bacteria, spores, and viruses.

Here are some effective disinfectants:

- *Chlorine (bleach)*—Mix 50 ml per liter (one ounce per quart) of water and soak items in this solution for thirty minutes. Do not use the granulated chlorine used in swimming pools.
- *Quartenary ammonium compounds*—These are available from your avian veterinarian under the brand name of Roccal. Use 2 ml of Roccal per liter of water.
- *Phenol-type disinfectants*—These are available from your avian veterinarian and are the most effective disinfectants against bacteria (pseudomonas), mycobacteria, candida, trichophyton fungi, and viruses such as Newcastle. The brand name is Environ One Stroke. Wear protective rubber gloves, because these compounds are corrosive to the skin. Also, keep these disinfectants away from your eyes.
- *Chlorhexidine*—This is available under the brand name of Nolvasan. Nolvasan is a very good virus disinfectant but is not effective against gram positive or pseudomonas bacteria.

TRAVELING WITH YOUR BIRD

Birds travel well if you plan ahead. If you are traveling by car, take your bird's favorite cage, cover, food, and toys along. It's a good idea to bring bottled water or water from home, since the varying mineral contents of water in new locations can cause your bird to pass loose droppings.

Do not leave your bird in a car during hot weather.

A general rule: Whenever making reservations at hotels or motels, check to be certain that pets are allowed.

If you want to take your bird with you on a plane, check with the airline ahead of time. Although reservations for your bird are not necessary, only one pet is allowed per cabin, so space must be requested in advance. Small birds may be carried on board in a cage, box, or other container. Large birds must travel with other large pets in specially designated areas of the plane. In both cases, there is a charge for each change of planes you must make en route to your destination. Check with your travel agent when taking your bird abroad. The fee for transporting your pet will depend on the city of destination and the size of your bird.

If your bird cannot go in the passenger section, use a flat crate with ventilation on one or more sides. It should have a slanted screen so that air flow cannot be cut off. Mark "Live Birds" on every side and indicate with arrows which side is "up." Carpet the "roof" of the container so that the bird cannot injure itself. Put a large amount of food in the crate. Use a slice of fruit for the water source.

Be aware that some cities in the United States (for instance, Albuquerque and Los Angeles) require a health certificate from a veterinarian declaring the bird free from disease. You should know that some foreign countries enforce quarantine periods which can last from one day to six months.

IF YOU GO AWAY

While you're gone, try to find someone to take care of your bird in *your* home. Changing location can be stressful to your bird. You might contact a local bird club to find someone to look after your bird during your absence, in your own home if possible, in theirs if not.

Should you decide to board your bird, choose a facility that is clean, quiet, and well ventilated. The staff should be familiar with bird care and should treat their temporary boarder with gentle care. If your veterinarian does not have boarding facilities, ask for a recommendation.

In general, you should call for reservations at least a week or two in advance (allow more time around holidays). Always leave your veterinarian's name and telephone number with the staff, as well as a number where you can be reached in case of emergency. Be sure that your bird is on its regular diet and that you provide *written* instructions detailing your bird's feeding schedule, habits, general care, and any special considerations the bird may require.

NUTRITION

Did your mother or grandmother ever complain that you "ate like a bird" because you did not eat *enough?* Well, they didn't know about birds. Birds burn up enormous amounts of energy very fast. In fact, some birds, such as the humming-bird, eat *twice* their weight in nectar daily. If you weigh 125 pounds, you would have to eat 250 pounds of food daily to keep up with the hummingbird!

Nutrition is the process of transforming food into living tissue. Without a complete and balanced diet, your bird will not grow properly, reproduce, maintain the health of all its body tissues, or fight infection.

Your bird's wild relatives spend most of the day feeding and looking for food, but your bird just hops on its perch and *expects* (rightfully so) that you will supply its food needs. It is your responsibility to provide your bird with a nourishing, varied, well-balanced diet. The following section will help you provide the complete and balanced diet that your bird's wild relatives search for daily.

FOOD FOR THOUGHT

If you want a happy, healthy bird, you must provide a well-balanced variety of food. The formulated pellet should be the keystone of your bird's diet. It is available from your avian veterinarian or pet store.

Pellet-Diet Manufacturers:

Mini-Friends
Purina Mills
800 Chouteau Avenue
St. Louis, MO 63164

Lafeber Company
R.R. #2
Odel, IL 60460

Zeigler Bros., Inc.
P.O. Box 95
Gardners, PA 17324

Roudybush
P.O. Box 331
Davis, CA 95617-0331

The pellet food seems to be well balanced. It has the additional advantages of being dust- and hull-free and is available in medicated forms from your veterinarian if your bird should get sick.

Converting Your Bird from a Seed to a Pellet Diet

Most parrots readily consume pellet bird food. However, a few, especially the older birds, are sometimes so behaviorally ingrained to hulling seeds that they are reluctant to eat unfamiliar food. For birds that don't readily consume new foods, these suggestions will help convert them to eating pellets.

STEP A: Day 1–Day 3
Offer pellets in feeders and sprinkle approximately one-half teaspoon of food per bird on the cage floor. Empty the feeder daily and refill with fresh food. Feed only pellets; do not offer seeds or provide any other supplementation.
STEP B: Day 4–Day 6
If your birds have not converted to pellets by day 3, remove feed and replace with a mixture of equal parts of pellets and seeds for the next three days. Then convert back exclusively to pellets on day 7.
STEP C: Day 7
Repeat step A and continue this process as necessary.

After completing two cycles of this familiarization process, almost all birds should be converted. If your bird(s) still refuse to change over, feed equal portions of seeds and pellets. Over time, the ratio of seeds to pellets can be gradually reduced, and the birds will eventually convert.

Selecting Appropriate Foods

Even birds on the well-formulated pellet diets need *variety*. Every day, select food products from each of the basic four food groups recommended by the Association of Avian Veterinarians.

Grains—Breads and Cereal Group
Recommended foods in this group include

Whole wheat bread
Cooked brown rice
Commercial monkey biscuit
Other whole-grain products

Fresh Vegetables and Fruits Group
Fresh dark green or yellow vegetables alone can account for 45 percent of your bird's daily food intake. Fruits can make up 2 percent of the daily intake. Make sure that the fruits and vegetables are washed thoroughly to eliminate pesticides.

Vegetables:

Broccoli	Parsley
Carrots	Pumpkin
Collard greens	Sweet potato
Corn on the cob	Tomatoes
Endive	Winter squash
Kale	

Fruits:

Apples	Grapes
Apricots	Oranges
Bananas	Papaya
Cantaloupe	

Meat Group

Meat provides protein and fat. Meat can make up 2 percent of the daily intake. Beef, chicken (it won't make your bird a cannibal), tuna, other fish, hard boiled or scrambled eggs, mature legumes (peanuts, chick peas, or navy, lima, or kidney beans) are appreciated.

Dairy Group

Birds do enjoy a *small* amount of yogurt, cottage cheese, and hard cheeses. Dairy products provide protein and calcium.

Use your imagination. My yellow-naped Amazon, named Cacul, likes his daily piece of pizza (provides cheese and tomato) or whole-wheat bread with peanut butter. He likes to "wash it down" with a piece of apple.

Other Feeding Tips

Soft foods such as sweet potato and peanut butter are also good ways of "hiding" medication if needed—and a great way to give the daily vitamin and mineral supplement rather than mixing it in the drinking water. Soft foods spoil, especially in warm weather, so just leave the additive in the food for a few hours before changing it. Wash the bowls thoroughly.

Cuttlefish bone, white oyster shell, and mineral blocks are good sources of calcium and other minerals and should be given to your bird.

Feeding too much fresh fruit and vegetables can cause loose droppings.

Do not feed your bird raw egg white. This binds up *biotin* (a B vitamin), which is necessary for growth.

Be careful with cod-liver oil as a routine supplement. Too much can cause an excess vitamin A problem or a vitamin E deficiency.

If there are signs of illness (such as loose droppings), your bird should receive a vitamin-mineral supplement, because vitamins (especially the B vitamins) and minerals may not be absorbed or utilized properly. All breeding birds should receive a vitamin-mineral supplement as well as the recommended dietary supplement.

A lack of iodine can cause thyroid gland enlargement (especially in budgerigars). A well-balanced and varied diet will prevent this condition.

Some foods are wonderful for exercise and play: whole nuts, corn on the cob, pine cones, and coconuts.

Water

Water is essential to birds. It is obtained through metabolism of the food (especially fats) and liquids that your bird ingests. Fresh fruits and green vegetables are a primary source of water. Your bird also needs constant access to clean, fresh drinking water. You might consider using bottled water or boiled tap water for your bird. Our water supply contains fluoride, chlorine, and a Pandora's box of other chemicals that are probably not good for us and even worse for a one- to two-pound bird.

Be sure to supply fresh, clean water at all times. Milk, fresh fruit, and green vegetables will also be appreciated by your bird.

Grit

Seed eaters grind up their food in the muscular stomach (gizzard) with the help of a hard, insoluble material called *grit*. Commercial "bird grit," consisting of quartz and other natural ingredients, is available in pet stores. Veterinarians do not, however, agree whether or not grit is actually necessary for normal digestion.

Aviary birds get some grit when they have access to a soil floor.

Seeds

Monkeys need only bananas; dogs and cats need only meat; birds need only seeds to be healthy. Right? Wrong! Severe vitamin and mineral deficiencies would occur from such diets. Remember, a *varied* diet is most important for your bird's health.

Try to eliminate or restrict seeds in your bird's diet. Seed-type "bird foods" are poor diets and cause or contribute to many bird diseases if used exclusively. Their B vitamins are contained in the seed hulls (which the bird does not eat). Overfeeding of the "oil seeds" (sunflower, peanut) and lack of exercise will produce a "blimpy bird." The fat usually accumulates in the chest area.

If you want to feed your bird seeds, how do you know if they are "dead" or not nutritious? Sprout them! If less than 80 percent of the seeds sprout, they have spoiled.

Method: Place some seeds on a pan covered with a paper towel. Soak the seeds with water. Spray seeds daily to keep them moist. The seeds will start to sprout in three or four days. Once they sprout, you can keep them in the refrigerator for up to a week. Rinse them before feeding, as they are very *nutritious.* The amount of sprouts that can be fed daily are as follows:

Finches, canaries	¼ teaspoon
Budgerigars	1 teaspoon
Cockatiels	1 tablespoon
Larger parrots	2-4 tablespoons

There are different *qualities* of seeds; they are determined by such things as growing conditions (soil, fertilizers, rainfall, temperature) and when seeds are harvested and how they are stored. Buy your seeds from reputable dealers or companies.

Birds remove the shell from the seeds and eat the nutritious kernel. The shell may fall back into the feed cup. The next day the feed cup may look full, but it may contain *only shells.* Be sure to keep the feed cup full of fresh seeds.

A few other feeding hints:

• You eat your food in clean bowls and dishes. Your bird deserves the same care. Be sure to keep your bird's feeding cups and bowls clean.
• Be sure that the perches are not placed over the feed and water cups. Droppings in the food and water are not healthy.
• Rotate food and water locations and feed your bird a variety of foods. This will make it more adaptable to change and less "set in its ways."

In summary, your bird needs a complete and balanced diet. Birds that live in the wild are able to select their foods from the "garden cafeteria" of earth. Since *you* have the *responsibility* for a bird's care, you must provide a *varied* diet to ensure that your bird does not become marginally malnourished and thus unable to fight infections and illnesses.

Birds with Special Food Needs

Mynah Birds, Toucans, and Toucanettes • Commercial mynah bird pellets may not meet these birds' nutritional needs, so supplement from the meats group. Fresh fruit, peanut butter, and dog food should also be used. Soft foods should be changed frequently, because bacteria will be produced in a few hours.

Lories and Lorikeets • A nectar-type formula is used and is available from Neckton USA, Inc., 1917 Tyrone Blvd., St. Petersburg, FL 33710 (lory diet Premix).

A semiliquid diet of blended monkey biscuits, molasses, fresh apples, carrots, and water can be made at home. You can supplement with small seeds, sunflower seeds, fresh fruits, vegetables, mealworms, and fresh branches.

Because the diet contains a lot of sugar, change the solution and the bowls frequently to prevent bacterial growth.

Pigeons and Doves • Nutritional problems are rare among these birds. Feed them a commercial pigeon pellet diet. Most commercial pigeon grain rations should be supplemented with chicken layer pellets with 20 percent protein. You can add corn, peas, and greens daily. Grit, oyster shell mineral supplements, and some salt are also required.

Feeding Wild Birds

Sometimes an injured wild bird becomes an "overnight guest" at your house. Besides providing shelter and warmth, what should your guest be given to eat? What should you do?

Look at the beak. Birds having cone-shaped beaks are primarily seed eaters (such as sparrows, finches, pigeons, and cardinals); those with long, thin, pointed beaks are primarily insect eaters (such as titmice, mockingbirds, wrens, warblers, and vireos); those with strong, hooked beaks are primarily meat eaters (such as hawks and owls). You can also look for your guest's "picture" in a bird identification book.

Seed Eaters

Feed the bird as you would finches and canaries or use wild birdseed. Pigeons can be fed commercially available Purina Pigeon Chow.

Insect Eaters

Use the same diet as above, but make sure that most of it is canned or dry dog food, live mealworms, cooked meat (beef or chicken), and strained beef or chicken baby food. A good diet is a finely ground dry dog food, a small amount of ground mynah pellets, and some houseflies.

Meat Eaters

Feed the bird raw beef hearts or liver, chicken, milk, vitamin-mineral supplement, and bone meal.

Nectar Eaters

Mix sugar water (four parts water, one part sugar), with a vitamin-mineral supplement and a protein source such as Mull-Soy, Gevral, Esbilac (Borden's substitute bitches' milk), or Instant Breakfast powder. Honey and chopped fruit are appreciated.

Omnivorous Birds

This group—which includes crows, jays, blackbirds, and starlings—eats a wide variety of fruits and proteins. You can feed them the same foods, particularly fruit and seeds, that you would give to insect-eating birds.

A vitamin-mineral supplement, grit, and cuttlebone should be provided. (Crows, however, do not need grit or cuttlebone.) Of course, a wild bird should be allowed to continue traveling as soon as its strength has returned. Use the Decision Charts and read the section on public health problems whenever you find a sick or injured wild bird.

Feeding a Breeding Bird

Breeding birds should be kept on their usual diet, but seeds and soft foods high in protein and calcium should be increased so that healthy eggs with normal shells will be laid, and so that egg binding will not occur. Vigorous young should be produced, and your bird should remain healthy if you are attentive to the increased nutritional needs of your egg-laying bird.

Feeding a Fat Bird

See the Decision Chart on overweight birds in Chapter 8.

CLEANING AND PREENING

Birds spend many hours preening—making themselves look pretty. Preening involves using the beak to reattach separated barbs on the feathers and to put the feathers back in position.

Many birds, including most of the pet birds, have a preen gland near the tail base. When your bird preens, it may distribute the oil from the preen gland onto its feathers to help waterproof them and keep them healthy.

Wild birds practice feather and skin hygiene in familiar ways with water (like us) and in bizarre ways with such things as "dust" or "ant" baths. Some birds wash by standing in the rain—very simple and very inexpensive. Other birds like to roll in wet grass or leaves, and others (probably descendants of the "Mashuga bird")

like to roll around in dust. I suppose we could call this a "dry shampoo." Other birds such as starlings, orioles, and jays like to play with their food and take "ant baths." The birds will place ants under their tail and wing feathers. The "ant juice" is thought to keep external parasites away or to help keep the skin and feathers healthy.

There is fortunately no need to have an "ant bath" in your bird's room because all pet birds enjoy bathing with water.

Finches and canaries like to plop into a shallow saucer of water and wiggle around. They usually jump out quickly, shake off, and dive in quickly again—with little peeps of pleasure and gratitude. Special bird baths can be purchased that will keep the cage dry. Some water-shy birds can be coaxed by placing some wet greens in the bird bath. More water can be added to these same greens for the next bath. Those canaries and finches who like to "shower" instead of taking a bath thoroughly enjoy a light misting with a spray bottle.

All birds—budgerigars, cockatiels, lovebirds, Amazons, macaws, cockatoos— love baths or showers. Use *shallow* containers (to prevent drowning) or light water- mist sprays. Some birds just like to wiggle around in wet greens.

Nail Trimming

Birds that have the proper size perches and climbing surfaces usually keep their nails worn down. Long nails can get caught on objects or cause your bird to stand improperly. The tips of the forward and backward nails should not meet or overlap on the perch.

As suggested for the beak, you can trim your bird's nails with an ordinary fingernail, cuticle, or (for large birds) toenail clipper. White's Dog Nail Clipper also works well for large parrots. Trim just in front of the pink area, or *dermis,* which contains nerves and blood vessels. If the nail is dark and the pink area cannot be seen easily, shine a bright penlight through the nail to see where the dermis begins. Otherwise, just trim the tips of the nail.

A nail trimmed too short will bleed. A styptic pencil, styptic powder, or direct pressure with gauze or a clean cloth will stop the bleeding. A loss of a few drops of blood can be a "bucketful" to a small bird.

See the section on restraint (page 109) so that nail trimming will not be an unhappy experience for you or your bird. Hold the toe firmly but gently as you trim the nail. After the nail is trimmed, you can file it to smooth out the rough edges.

Beak Trimming

Nail, beak, and wing trimming can be done by you or your veterinarian. Proper nutrition, beak exercise (cuttlefish bone or lava stone), and climbing exercise for parrots should keep the beak in good shape. If, because of past injury or mite infestation, the beak grows long, it should be trimmed so that your bird can grasp and eat its food.

You can trim your bird's beak with an ordinary fingernail, cuticle, or (for large birds) toenail clipper, or White's Dog Nail Clipper. Shine a bright penlight through the beak to see where the blood vessel is located.

A beak trimmed too short will bleed. Follow the instructions in the section on restraint, and if bleeding occurs, the tips regarding nail trimming.

Wing Trimming

Wing trims prevent your bird from flying and also are helpful for taming and training.

There are many types of trims. The most popular and most attractive is clipping the feathers on one wing. All the primary flight and secondary feathers—except for three primaries at the tip and a few secondaries close to the body—are trimmed even with or a little shorter than the overlying tertiary (coverts). This unbalances most birds so that "lift-off" is not possible. Some birds need feathers on the other wing trimmed, too, to prevent flight. A few "super birds" may still have some flying ability with both wings clipped.

For the first trim you might want your avian veterinarian to show you how to handle your bird's wing.

If a blood feather (the quill is blue) is inadvertently cut, the entire feather must be removed (see "Bleeding," page 113.)

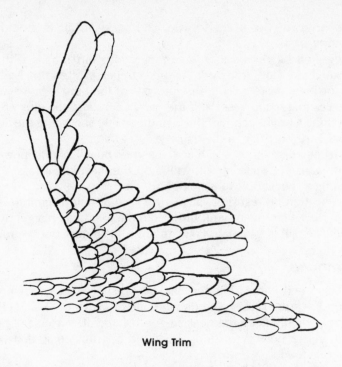

Wing Trim

Bye-Bye Birdy—The Great Escape

Trimming your bird's wings will prevent it from "flying the coop." If you do not want to trim the wings, make sure that all doors and windows are secured when you give your bird free-flight time.

You can be prepared for an escape by having handy an audio tape of your bird's calls, songs, or speech. Most birds will come home if you have patience and follow them with your tape playing, a cage, a net or towel, and possibly another bird of the same species—a decoy—in a separate cage, calling or squawking to your runaway friend.

Teach your bird to repeat its address. Recently, a parakeet was returned to its owner because it knew the proper address.

AEROBICS AND EXERCISE

Exercise is essential for *our* physical and mental health. If we don't get exercise, we may smoke too much, gain weight, or have temper tantrums and constant headaches. Exercise helps release this tension. Birds need exercise, too. Think

about what your bird would be doing in a wild state and then try to simulate the experience for it—provide exercise, companions, and time for free flight.

Physical Exercise

Wing Exercise

Your bird's cage should be long enough for reasonably long flights. The wings when fully extended should not hit the sides. The tail feathers should not touch the cage floor or sides when your bird turns.

Free-flight time should be part of your bird's routine. Birds love the exercise and the excitement of their extended home. Be sure to go over this checklist before letting your bird have its free-flight time.

- Remove all poisonous plants.
- Cover mirrors and windows so that your bird will not fly into them.
- Keep all doors closed and locked, so that an unexpected visitor doesn't open the door and allow your bird to take off for the wide-open country.
- If you must use the stove top when your bird is flying free, be sure to cover all pots and pans.
- Keep other pets (dogs and cats) out of the room during free-flight unless they are well socialized to birds.

- Small children can injure or kill small birds, and they can be injured by the large parrots. Always be present when children are enjoying the bird's free-flight time.
- Leave the cage door open so that your bird can return when it feels like it. A "special treat" will get your bird back to its cage when you want free-flight time to be over. Even with all these precautions, watch your bird closely during free-flight time. Members of the parrot family—chewers by trade—must be watched with extra care.

Toe Exercise

It is very important to provide clean, dry perches of various sizes to exercise your bird's toes and help keep the nails trim. Fruit trees (which have not been sprayed with chemicals) such as apple or pear are fine for perches, as are maple, willow, elm, ash, and nut trees. Oval perches are better than round perches.

Keep the perches dry and clean. Perches should be widely spaced and at different levels for exercise value. Do not place one perch directly under another perch, since not even a bird likes to get a dropping on the head.

The larger parrots should be provided with a T-perch. Your bird should *not* be chained to the perch. This is cruel and may cause a broken leg if your bird is frightened and struggles to escape.

Beak Exercise

All birds like to rub their beaks on their perches for exercise, and some rub their beaks on their perches during courtship.

The cuttlefish bone or lava stone (for larger parrots) provides calcium and other minerals and is also important in exercising the beak and keeping it sharp and trim.

Members of the parrot family love to climb. They use their beaks to climb along perches and cage bars, and up your arm. The beak is also a very important way for birds to "feel" their environment and to show their affection. Tree branches or lumber will have to be replaced constantly since chewing is a parrot's favorite pastime.

Mental Exercise

Birds need games and toys. They need to hear sounds and see objects. In other words, they need mental stimulation, or they may go as "crazy as a loon," or become as "dumb as a dodo bird."

Budgerigars

Provide a few toys and playthings for mental stimulation but don't overcrowd the cage. Budgerigars like mirrors, ladders, swings, and small bells. Do not hang anything by a string in the cage. Your bird can get tangled in it and be seriously injured. Mental stimulation also comes from having a friendly companion (you or another budgerigar) and free-flight time.

Cockatiels

These birds love mirrors, bells, and ladders for exercise and mental stimulation. Providing free-flight time or wiring a perch to the top of the cage will stimulate your bird and bring out its playful and responsive personality. Mental stimulation also comes from having a friendly companion (you or another cockatiel).

Larger Parrots (Amazons, Macaws, and Cockatoos)

Such birds should be *uncaged* most of the time to make them playful and responsive. Wiring a tree branch or lumber to the top of the cage or using a T-perch will make your bird feel happy and at home. The larger parrots also enjoy wooden spools, wooden chew blocks, small cowbells, rawhide bones, or Nylabones (made for dogs). Clipping a wing and keeping forbidden objects away from your free-perching bird will prevent injuries and furniture damage.

Remember, *you* are responsible for your feathered companion's physical and mental health. If you were kept in a small room for the rest of your life and given your food but no companionship, how would you feel and what would you do? Think about this and try to make your bird's life as pleasant as possible. You will be greatly rewarded with a happy bird that will give you years of joy and pleasure.

If you have provided for your bird's physical and mental needs, you should have a happy, friendly bird and a good pet. But always be on the lookout for any developing problems and try to find their cause.

A few signs of unhappiness

- Agitated hopping or flying from perch to perch
- Feather picking
- Toe chewing
- Larger parrots may make constant, repetitive movements, such as figure eights, bowing, or side-to-side motions—with their heads and bodies.
- Excessive aggression and constant squawking
- No interest in playing, singing, talking, or chewing (of course, these may also be signs of illness)

TAMING AND TRAINING

Since your bird is going to be a member of your family, you should know how to tame and train it. You will be rewarded with a well-behaved companion who will

57

give you many years of pleasure. The taming and training period can be divided into three categories: getting acquainted, training techniques, and talking.

Getting Acquainted

Put yourself in your bird's place: You have been taken away from your family and placed in a strange cage in a new room with different sights and sounds and no place to hide. There are huge, unfeathered creatures with no beaks making strange noises in front of your cage. How would you feel? Frightened, of course!

As you can see, the first few days should be devoted to getting acquainted. It is very important that you move slowly and talk quietly to your new family member. In a few days, you will probably see that your bird is less frightened—it won't jump from perch to perch, squawk, hiss, or fluff its feathers as much when you approach or stand near its cage. Try to learn your bird's body language and "speech"—its signs of aggression as well as its signs of trust. Try to imitate its "trusting" sounds.

Training Techniques

After a few days, your bird will still not trust you completely but will tolerate your presence. This is the time to start hand taming your bird. For the next week, try to show your bird that perching on your hand or on a stick can be fun. A bare hand can be used for finches, canaries, and budgerigars, but leather work gloves should be worn with the smaller parrots. A stick of broom-handle thickness works well for parrots, especially macaws and cockatoos. Since your bird will feel more secure in its cage, start the hand or stick training in the cage, with a few fifteen-minute sessions each day. Using slow movements and a calm, reassuring voice, introduce your hand or stick into the cage. By gently pushing up where the chest joins the legs, you can get your bird to jump onto your finger or your stick. Parrots grasp with their beaks before climbing up on objects, so don't be frightened when the beak comes before the legs. Once you have succeeded in using the stick method for your parrot, the next step is to ease your stick-holding hand under your bird's feet while talking softly and gently. Now offer small bits of food with your free hand to distract your bird, then simply slide your hand over, drop the stick softly—and the bird is on *your* hand. That contact is a good feeling—instant communication—like shaking hands with someone. Continue to reassure your bird as it ponders its new perch—your hand.

After you have hand tamed your bird, other family members should be encouraged to handle it and feed it treats so that it will become accustomed to many people.

You are now well on your way to having a well-socialized, hand-tamed pet. Once your bird feels comfortable on your hand, you should slowly and with gentle reassurances remove it from the cage. It will probably jump off your hand or grab for the bars first. But with patience and determination and with a reassuring voice and a few treats, you will be successful. Again, these sessions should be no more than fifteen minutes, two or three times a day, and they should be handled by only one person so that your bird does not get confused or frightened. The room should be quiet, and all distractions such as toys, mirrors, and bells should be removed during training sessions.

During training sessions:

- Close and cover all windows
- Close and (if possible) lock all doors
- Cover boiling liquids. Better yet, don't cook at this time.

Once your bird is hand tamed, it will beg you to take it for rides around on your hand, arm, shoulder, or the top of your head! If your bird tries to nip at your hand, turn your fingers away and push your bird's chin away with your other hand. Some birds *do* learn the meaning of the word *no*. Never hit your bird. They do not understand this type of punishment, but they do respond to gentleness and patience.

If your bird flies off your finger when you first take it out of the cage, don't lunge for it like an outfielder chasing a ball. Simply wait until it has perched and then slowly and quietly offer your hand, a stick, or even the cage to it. Offering some treat or fruit is also helpful. If this doesn't work, don't worry. Just leave the cage door open with some fresh goodies inside, and your bird will return to the cage on its own time. If this doesn't work, wait until dark. Your bird will sleep, and you can try your "salesmanship" again in the morning.

Talking

Birds of the parrot family—budgerigars, cockatiels, African greys, macaws, and cockatoos, for example—can learn to "talk." Actually, they mimic or imitate your speech, the calls and songs of other birds, and even sounds around the house, such as the chimes of a grandfather clock, a banging door, or the ring of a telephone. They seem to enjoy this wonderful talent, and so do their owners. The neighbors are another story.

- You should start "speech classes" only after your bird has been tamed and is accustomed to you.
- In general, males seem to learn more words and sounds faster than females, but there are many females who can talk circles around the opposite sex.
- Younger birds are easier to teach, but you may still be able to teach an "old bird new tricks" with patience and kindness.
- It is best to remove toys, mirrors, and food cups during the classes.

- Birds like routine. Give the lessons at the same time each day (before the cage cover is off in the morning and after it is replaced in the evening, for example).
- Single birds are easier to teach than those that have company.
- Each lesson should be about fifteen minutes long.
- Be sure the "classroom" is quiet, without television, radios, or stereos blaring. If there are other people present, they should be quiet as well.
- Birds seem to respond better to the voices of females or children.
- It may take one month to one year to teach your bird to speak. Once it utters its first word or phrase, others will come easier and faster. In fact, your bird will love its newfound talent so much that it will rapidly pick up more words. Some birds never learn to talk but make pleasant pets anyhow.
- The best "first words" are your bird's name and then its address. Lost birds *have* been returned home because they "remembered" where they lived.
- Short words and phrases are best for lessons. A new word should be repeated slowly many times. It should also be repeated whenever you, other family members, or friends pass the cage or T-stand.
- To save your time, you can purchase a bird-training record or make your own tape recording of the word or phrase repeated over and over. Of course, a "live" performance by you is important after your bird has listened to the recording.
- Some parrots can graduate to the "school of clean tricks"—learning to put objects in containers, ring bells for a reward, do somersaults, or other delightful show-stopping stunts! If you watch your bird's natural antics, you can adapt simple stunts around them. Be careful not to use any materials or toys that may injure your bird.

PARASITES

A parasite obtains its nutrition from your bird and gives nothing in return except possible illness. This one-sided relationship has been under attack by concerned bird owners, veterinarians, and pharmaceutical companies.

Reading this section and the Decision Charts will make you aware of any parasite problem your bird may have, whether you should treat it at home or go to your veterinarian, and help you prevent the parasite from finding a home on or in your bird's body.

If you purchased your bird from a reputable, conscientious breeder, it will probably not have parasites. If your bird was imported or lives in an outdoor aviary with exposure to wild birds or to a dirt floor, parasites are more likely. Only some of the most common parasites of pet birds will be discussed here.

Skin Parasites

Scaly face or scaly leg mite (Cnemidocoptes)

Who gets them?

Any bird. Budgerigars, lovebirds, and canaries are the most commonly affected pet birds.

What do they look like?

They are microscopic, round "bugs" with short, stumpy legs.

How are they spread?

Birds seem to get the mites from their parents when they are nestlings (babies in the nest).

What is their life cycle?

The mite spends its entire development on the bird. It burrows into the skin and feather follicles, then lays its eggs in the tunnels that are formed from the burrowing. The new mites continue the interconnecting tunnels into new skin and feather follicles.

Some birds may have the mites and never get "scaly leg" or "scaly face" disease. Their immune system seems to protect them.

Are there any signs to look for?

White, scaly deposits. The most common areas affected are the eyelids, beak corners, legs, toes, and around the vent. The mite can damage the beak's growth plate and cause a crooked, deformed beak that will have to be trimmed frequently so that your bird can eat.

How are they diagnosed?

Physical examination. The white, scaly deposits have a characteristic appearance. Microscopic examination of scrapings from the deposits will show the mites.

What is the treatment?

At home, plain mineral oil applied with a cotton-tipped applicator can be used daily to soften the deposits if the disease is not too far along. Use a rotary motion to break down the deposits. The oil will loosen the deposits and also clog the mites' air holes. Do not get too much oil on the feathers.

This may cause the bird to become ill or die from chilling.

Your doctor may prescribe an ointment or give an injection of Ivermectin.

Clean the cage, perches, and toys. Although the mite may no longer be on the bird, it may live for a while in small deposits that have fallen off.

Isolate the bird from your other birds until the white deposits are gone.

Can they be prevented?

New birds should be isolated and checked for thirty days before introducing them to your other birds.

Feather Mites

(such as the red mite or the depluming scabies mite)

Who gets them?

Feather mites that cause skin and feather problems are not a common problem in modern aviaries. Not all feather mites are bad. Your bird can also have some "harmless" feather mites that live snugly with it and never cause a problem.

What do they look like?

Moving, tiny red specks (which is the red mite that causes problems).

How are they spread?

They are brought in by an infected bird or by wild birds visiting an outdoor aviary. These mites hide under feed and water cups, nests, perch corners, and droppings. They feed at night on your bird's blood.

What is their life cycle?

The female lays her eggs in cracks and crevices after sucking your bird's blood. The eggs hatch in twenty-four hours in a warm, moist environment. The baby red mite sucks blood and grows into an adult in a few days.

Are there any signs to look for?	Restlessness, severe scratching and feather picking, extensive skin irritation; nestlings may become weak and die from anemia caused by the blood-sucking mites.
How are they diagnosed?	The small, moving, red dots can be seen on the underside of a white cloth placed over the cage for the night. You can also sneak up on them at night. The little red dots can be seen on the birds or perches by shining a bright light into the cage. A magnifying lens will make them more visible.
What is the treatment?	Your veterinarian will prescribe an appropriate chemical to use in treating your bird and its cage. The nesting materials and perches should be discarded and replaced with new ones.
Can they be prevented?	New birds should be isolated and checked for thirty days before introducing them to your other birds.
	Purchase your birds from a reliable, reputable dealer or breeder.
	If you have an outdoor aviary, minimize the exposure that your birds will have to wild birds.

Lice

Who gets them?	Not very common in pet birds unless they come in contact with wild birds.
What do they look like?	Tiny white oval specks that are seen best with a magnifying glass.
How are they spread?	They can spread to your pet bird if they come in contact with wild birds in an outdoor aviary or near an open window. But as lice are extremely host and species specific, the chances of this happening are very small.

What is their life cycle?

They spend their whole life cycle on the bird. The cluster of eggs laid are called *nits,* and they can usually be seen attached to the feather as white clusters. After hatching, the young lice go through transformations called nymph stages before reaching adulthood in about three weeks. They are passed to another bird by direct contact, especially during mating and nesting.

Are there any signs to look for?

Restlessness, constant feather picking, scratching and feather ruffling, and skin irritation (especially on the head). Feather damage and a "moth-eaten" appearance may result.

How are they diagnosed?

By finding the tiny white eggs, nymphs, or adult lice attached to the feathers.

What is the treatment?

An insecticide containing rotenone or pyrethrin will be prescribed by your veterinarian.

Clean and fumigate (with the above) the cage and discard the perches, nests, and nest boxes. Replace with new ones.

Can they be prevented?

New birds should be isolated and checked for thirty days before introducing them to your other birds.

Purchase your birds from a reliable, respectable dealer or breeder.

Fleas and Ticks

Fleas (thin, wingless, brown insects), and ticks (fat, brown, bean-shaped bugs) are not very common on pet birds. They may be seen in birds kept in an outdoor aviary. Using a topical insecticide (prescribed by your veterinarian) and fumigating the cage and then washing it down will stop this problem. Ticks can be removed by grasping them with your gloved fingers or tweezers close to where they are embedded and firmly pulling them out. By the way, a tick does *not* get its whole body under the skin!

Respiratory System Parasites

Gapeworms (syngamus)

Who gets them?	All birds. Not very common in pet birds.
What do they look like?	Tiny, blood-red, threadlike worms in the breathing tubes.
How are they spread?	From eating the eggs or larvae in the soil. Earthworms or snails may also harbor the baby gapeworm, which may in turn be eaten by birds.
What is their life cycle?	The female lays eggs in the trachea. They are coughed up, swallowed, and passed out in the droppings. Other birds swallow the eggs that are in the soil or eat earthworms, slugs, and other insects that have ingested the eggs.
	The larva migrates to the lungs and trachea and becomes an adult gapeworm.
Are there any signs to look for?	"Gaping" or gasping for air (caused by partial blockage of the breathing tubes by the worms and by the inflammation and pneumonia they produce); coughing, starvation, and anemia—since these worms are bloodsuckers.
How are they diagnosed?	By microscopic exam of a stool sample containing the eggs.
What is the treatment?	Ivermectin.
Can they be prevented?	All new birds should have their stool samples examined. Birds in outdoor aviaries with dirt floors are more susceptible to gapeworms.

Digestive System Parasites

Roundworms

Who gets them?	All birds. One of the most common parasites.

What do they look like?	Long, thin, white, round worms.
How are they spread?	Ingestion of the worm eggs.
What is the life cycle?	The eggs are swallowed, and the larvae mature in the intestinal wall and the intestine proper into long, thin, white worms.
Are there any signs to look for?	The worms seem to live nicely with their "host," but on occasion poor plumage, weight loss, loose droppings, and even intestinal blockage may be evident.
How are they diagnosed?	Check successive stool samples.
What is the treatment?	Piperazine, fenbendazole, thiabendazole, Ivermectin, or pyrantel.
Can they be prevented?	Keep environment sanitary. Remove droppings from aviary. Wash concrete flooring of aviary often. Control mice and cockroaches. Have your veterinarian check at least two or three successive stool samples of a new bird and worm your bird, if necessary.

Capillaria ("threadworms")

Who gets them?	All birds. Among the pet birds, canaries and parakeets may have them.
What do they look like?	Microscopic and threadlike.
How are they spread?	The worm eggs are swallowed.
What is their life cycle?	The eggs pass out in the droppings and are swallowed by other birds. The larva becomes an adult in the crop or intestine.
Are there any signs to look for?	Decreased appetite, weight loss, loose droppings, regurgitation, and poor plumage.
How are they diagnosed?	Check successive stool samples.

What is the treatment? | Levamisole or pyrantel.

Can they be prevented? | Keep environment sanitary. Have your veterinarian check at least two or three successive stool samples of a new bird before allowing contact with your other birds.

Trichomonas

Who gets them? | This parasite causes a disease called "canker" in pigeons and "frounce" in falcons. It has also been diagnosed in canaries and finches.

What do they look like? | A microscopic protozoan that has a flapping membrane and a tail.

How are they spread? | In the droppings. In the United States it is mainly a pigeon problem, and pet birds in outdoor aviaries would probably be most susceptible.

What is their life cycle? | The trichomonas organisms are ingested and spend their life in the throat, crop, intestine, or liver.

Are there any signs to look for? | Cheesy-like material or hard masses in the mouth or throat area; weakness, decreased appetite, loose droppings, shortness of breath.

How are they diagnosed? | Smears of the cheesy material.

What is the treatment? | Metronidazole.

Can they be prevented? | Prevent contact between outdoor aviary birds and wild birds. Keep the water clean.

Coccidiosis

Who gets them? | Any bird, although this is not much of a problem in pet birds.

What do they look like? | Microscopic protozoans.

How are they spread?

In the droppings.

What is their life cycle?

The eggs are ingested, and the protozoan matures in the intestine.

Are there any signs to look for?

They usually do not cause illness when present, but occasionally will cause decreased appetite, weight loss, and loose (sometimes bloody) droppings.

How are they diagnosed?

Check successive stool samples.

What is the treatment?

Sulfa drugs are effective. Time allows immunity to develop.

Can they be prevented?

Good sanitation is essential. Check successive stool samples of a new bird before allowing contact with your other birds.

Giardia

Who gets them?

Any bird. Especially cockatiels, budgerigars, lovebirds, grey-cheek parakeets, poultry, and waterfowl.

What do they look like?

Microscopic protozoan.

How are they spread?

In the droppings or contaminated food and water supplies.

What is their life cycle?

The cysts are ingested, and the protozoan matures in the intestinal tract.

Are there any signs to look for?

Diarrhea, "cow-plop" stools, flaky dry skin, and persistent feather picking. Many of these birds are incorrectly diagnosed as "psychological" feather pickers. In fact, the itching is caused by malabsorption of fats, proteins, and vitamins and an allergy to giardia. Even a shifting leg lameness seen in cockatiels and budgerigars can be associated with giardiasis.

How are they diagnosed?	The fecal trichrome stain is the most reliable test. A *fresh* (less than five minutes old) stool sample is required.
What is the treatment?	Metronidazole and vitamins.
Can they be prevented?	Good sanitation is essential. Contaminated water must be boiled. Rats and other sources of giardia must be controlled in aviaries.

SOME IMPORTANT BIRD DISEASES

Psittacosis (Parrot fever, chlamydiosis)

What causes it?	Chlamydia psittaci, a bacterialike organism.
What species are affected?	All birds and animals. Budgerigars, cockatiels, cockatoos, wild pigeons, and doves may be carriers.
How is it spread?	By feces, fecal-contaminated food and water, and respiratory secretions. From sick or convalescent birds (can shed for many months) or well-bird carriers. Some birds can be carriers with no outward signs of illness for as long as ten years! The organism can live for a long time in a dry form outside the body in fecal or feather dust.
Are there any signs to look for?	Ruffled or poor feathering, listlessness, decreased appetite, weight loss, closing of the eyes, conjunctivitis, nasal discharge, labored breathing, loose green droppings, or central nervous system signs (tremors, head twisting, and convulsions).
How is it diagnosed?	A fluorescent antibody blood test, isolation of the organism in the feces, or by biopsy. Other blood tests and radiographs (X-rays) may be helpful. A high white count, an abnormal liver test, and an enlarged spleen and liver are frequently seen.

What is the treatment?

Doxycycline is the treatment of choice.

How can it be prevented?

Isolate and/or treat newly purchased birds for forty-five days. Mop frequently, clean cages with Roccal-D. Avoid overcrowding. Purchase birds from breeders of psittacosis-free stock. If you board your bird, consider it a "new bird" again regarding possible exposure to psittacosis.

Can humans get psittacosis?

Yes. It can feel like a mild flu or fever, and headaches, cough, and an atypical pneumonia may be present. Complications include encephalitis, heart inflammation, and death. It is treated with doxycycline.

Virus Diseases

Psittacine Beak and Feather Disease

What causes it?

Probably a virus.

What species are affected?

All parrot species. First seen in cockatoos.

How is it spread?

Not known.

Are there any signs to look for?

Progressive feather loss and replacement with deformed feathers; "beak rot"; the skin heals slowly from wounds. The immune system is suppressed, so the bird is susceptible to other infections. Poor weight gain.

How is it diagnosed?

Physical examination and microscopic examination of new feathers. Biopsy of the skin or beak. A fluorescent antibody test will probably be available soon.

What is the treatment?

Stimulating the immune system, controlling secondary infections with antimicrobials, giving supportive medications (vitamins, minerals), and controlling pain. Autogenous bacteria vaccines. Soft-food diets.

Proventricular Dilation ("macaw wasting disease")

What causes it?	Probably a virus (paramyxovirus) that attacks the nervous system to the digestive tract.
What species are affected?	Macaws, cockatoos, and possibly other species.
How is it spread?	Not known.
Are there any signs to look for?	Weight loss, regurgitation (vomiting), diarrhea, undigested food particles in the droppings, listlessness, and variable neurologic signs.
How is it diagnosed?	Radiograph (X-ray) shows an enlarged proventriculus ("stomach"); biopsy of the stomach. A test for the virus would be helpful.
What is the treatment?	Surgical removal of the stomach contents. Soft-food diet. Supportive care.

Reovirus

What causes it?	Reovirus.
What species are affected?	All species, especially the African grey.
How is it spread?	Probably in feces and respiratory secretions and in the egg.
Are there any signs to look for?	Nonspecific. Weight loss, shortness of breath, incoordination, yellow urates, swollen abdomen.
How is it diagnosed?	Virus culture, liver biopsy.
What is the treatment?	Supportive care.
How can it be prevented?	Quarantine "new birds" for six to twelve weeks. Practice good hygiene and disinfection.

Avian Pox

What causes it?	Pox virus.

What species are affected?	Amazons, budgerigars, lovebirds, canaries, and pigeons.
How is it spread?	By mosquitoes, pecking, feces, and skin or feather quill.
Are there any signs to look for?	Skin sores on unfeathered areas (on eyelids, for example, or wing webs in lovebird pox); sores and thickened grey-brown cheesy material in the mouth and throat. A watery discharge and eyelid inflammation (conjunctivitis) may be the only sign. Sudden death may occur in some birds.
How is it diagnosed?	Biopsy. Virus culture. (Avian pox can look similar to trichomoniasis, fungal infections such as candidiasis or aspergellosis, vitamin A deficiency, or the herpes virus of pigeons or Amazons.)

Pacheco's Disease

What causes it?	Herpes virus that has a specific liking for the liver.
What species are affected?	Most parrot species. Conures, Amazons, and macaws can be carriers and not show signs of disease.
How is it spread?	In the feces and from the respiratory tract.
Are there any signs to look for?	The signs are nonspecific. The smaller parrots (parakeets, lovebirds), some Amazons, and cockatoos may only show weakness a few hours before death. Macaws and some cockatoos may become lethargic, regurgitate, and have diarrhea. They may show increased thirst and recover. The longer the course of the disease, the better the chance for survival.
How is it diagnosed?	Virus isolation, liver biopsy. Veterinarians need to rule out lead poisoning, psittacosis, Newcastle disease, and salmonella.
What is the treatment?	No specific treatment—just supportive care: warmth, fluids, antibiotics, tube feeding, and vita-

min C. An antiherpes virus drug, Acyclovir, may be useful.

How can it be prevented?

Quarantine "new birds" for six to twelve weeks. Virus, bacterial, parasitic, and serum tests can be done at this time. Since conures are asymptomatic carriers, it may be wise to separate them from other species. Strict hygiene and disinfection are very important.

Newcastle Disease

What causes it?

Paramyxovirus.

What species are affected?

All birds.

How is it spread?

Feces, respiratory secretions.

Are there any signs to look for?

Central nervous system signs (twisted neck, limb paralysis, tremors, convulsions), respiratory or digestive disease. Sudden death may occur. This is a serious disease that could wipe out the poultry industry in this country. A suspected bird should be tested.

How is it diagnosed?

Virus isolation from organs or feces.

What is the treatment?

Supportive care.

How can it be prevented?

Vaccination is recommended for aviaries, breeding farms, and zoo collections.

Summary

Viruses probably play an important role in avian illness. Gram negative bacteria, chlamydia (psittacosis), and salmonella illnesses, in some cases, may be triggered by virus infections. Wartlike growths on African greys, macaws, and cockatoos; inflammation of the trachea (breathing tubes) in Amazons; bleeding disorders of conures; and some hepatitis and pancreatitis cases among budgerigars and lovebirds are virus related, as are some reproductive problems like "dead in the shell" (a condition possibly caused by herpes virus). The availability of serum tests for diagnosis, vaccinations, and antiviral agents will be a major step in avian medicine.

Going
to the
Veterinarian

Veterinarians fall into one of the following categories in their treatment of birds and their attitudes towards them.

- "Bring your pet in. I love seeing birds and have a special interest in them. I will try to help you."
- "I don't know much about birds, but I'll get my books out and we'll work together trying to help your bird."
- "I don't know much about birds, but Dr. Smith has a special interest in them. Why don't you see him (or her)?"
- "I don't see birds."

You may also encounter the type who says nothing, knows nothing about birds, and has no interest in them but will see you for the income.

Try to find a doctor in the first category. It takes four years of premedical or preveterinary school and four years of veterinary school for a person to become a veterinarian (with a small but increasing amount of this time spent on bird medicine). The important thing is that graduate veterinarians are given the "mental tools" to work on any animal. Any doctor who has a thirst for knowledge, a reverence for all life, and an interest in animals—birds, reptiles, guinea pigs, rabbits, or whatever—should be able to help you keep your bird healthy through good preventive-care information and whatever medical and surgical care that may be needed. In fact, most illnesses that afflict birds are the same as, and require the same treatment as, the ones that afflict us, or our dogs, cats, horses, or cows. All doctors should also know their limitations—and when to refer you to a specialist (yes, there are veterinary specialists—a chart of specialties appears on page 76). Check the phone book for a doctor with a special interest in avian medicine or contact the Association of Avian Veterinarians (page 15) for a doctor in your area.

EVALUATING THE VETERINARIAN

Selecting a veterinarian for your bird deserves the same consideration as choosing a family physician. Ask your neighbors, friends, local bird breeders, or pet shops for recommendations. You could also call your local zoo or veterinary school and ask if they know of area veterinarians with a special interest in birds.

The most important factor in the selection is your confidence in that person. Consider the following points when evaluating and selecting a veterinarian.

1. **Is the office clean and well equipped?**
   As far as bird medicine is concerned, your doctor should have at least the minimum equipment and supplies: an *infant incubator* or some

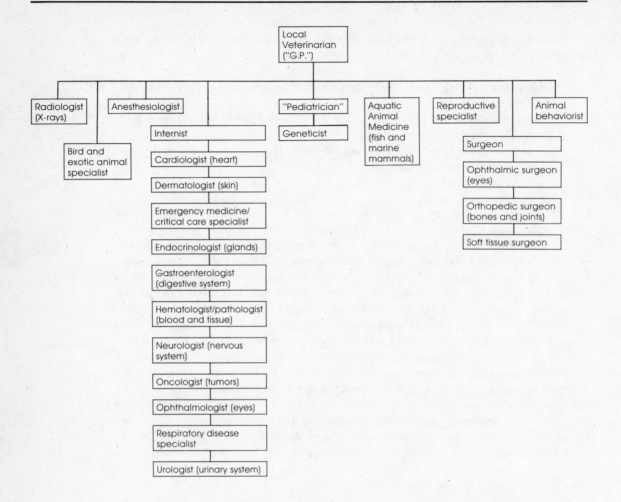

means (such as heat lamps) of keeping your bird warm if it needs to be hospitalized; *oxygen;* special *"bird syringes"* (called microliter syringes) since birds require such small amounts of injected medications; *towels or work gloves* for restraint of the larger parrots; *feeding tubes,* in case your bird needs to be force-fed; *opthalmic surgical instruments* small enough for bird surgery; *gas anesthesia machine; X-ray machine; heating pad* (a K-pad, with warm water circulating is the best) to keep your bird warm during surgery; and a *blood analyzer machine*, although some laboratories are now able to perform important bird tests on very small quantities of blood.

2. **Is the doctor on an appointment system?**

    This reduces your waiting time considerably, makes the reception area less crowded, and makes your doctor less rushed. Thoughtful veterinarians will schedule birds for the quietest part of their schedule, because a sick bird will be under severe stress in a crowded reception area with cats hissing, dogs barking, telephones ringing, and doors slamming.

3. **Can you take a tour of the clinic at a time convenient for the doctor or the staff?**

    Most veterinarians will be proud to show you their facilities and the special equipment and supplies needed for treating birds.

4. **Does the veterinarian take an appropriate medical history?**

    All veterinarians have been trained to organize background information in a logical, concise, and accurate way. This is called "taking the medical history," and it is extremely important in the care and treatment of birds. A history is divided into the major problem, the present illness, a review of systems, and the past medical history. Emergencies (such as injuries), simple problems, and well-bird exams may not require many questions by the doctor.

The Major Medical Problem

Before your visit, write down all the problems that your bird is having so that you won't leave out any important details. The major problem should appear first: "Big Bird's *droppings* have been loose."

The Current Illness

Your veterinarian will want to establish the progression of the current illness. This means that you must observe your bird very carefully at home so that you can provide all the relevant information. Again, organize your thoughts so that all the important facts are given.

Identify each problem without unnecessary details and let the doctor pick up from there.

"Three days ago, Big Bird, my parakeet, began having loose droppings—very watery. He also began drinking a lot more water. I measured it—four teaspoons daily! [one-half to one teaspoon daily is normal]. His appetite is very good, but his breastbone is starting to show [weight loss]."

Other information that may be useful is any medication that your bird took before and during the current illness. Bring the medications (or their names) with you. If X-rays or laboratory tests have been performed for past illnesses or for the current illness at another veterinarian's office, have the results phoned or sent to your current veterinarian. If your bird is allergic to any medication, make sure the doctor knows this.

Other information that may be requested by your doctor:

- How old is your bird? What sex is it?
- How long have you had the bird?
- Where did it come from?
- Does your bird chew on things around the house or in its cage? Tree branches, plaster, paint, plastics, houseplants? Do you use aerosols near its cage?
- What is its daily routine? Is there a change in the environment—new sounds, new house, redecorating? Does it get enough exercise and companionship?
- Where is your bird housed? In what room? What kind of heat or air conditioning do you have?
- Do you have any other birds or pets? Have they been ill recently?
- Have you had a cold recently? Do you kiss your bird?
- Do you wash your hands before handling your bird?
- What is your bird's diet? How is the food stored?

The Review of Systems

Your veterinarian will ask you specific questions related to the feathers, respiratory system, crop, stomach, intestines, urinary system, muscles, bones, nervous system, eyes, nose, and throat. The questions will help your doctor find the systems involved in the current illness.

The Past Medical History

In many cases previous illnesses, injuries, surgical procedures, or medications are related to the current illness. Be sure that you keep *complete* records. "She had a white liquid" does not tell your doctor anything. Be sure that all medications are *named* when dispensed. And write the name and amount used in your bird's home health record. Dates of illnesses (both those treated and those not requiring a visit), dates of and reasons for hospitalization (with a compete list of all lab tests, X-rays, and drugs administered) and surgical procedures (including the anesthesia used) should be recorded. You would be surprised how many times this information is relevant to the current illness.

5. **Does your veterinarian do a complete physical examination?**

Your bird deserves a *complete* physical examination even during well-bird visits. Many early problems can be picked up at these semiannual or annual visits. A thorough medical history and physical examination will probably suggest the diagnosis to most competent veterinarians.

All veterinarians establish their own order in the physical exam. Most doctors will start by observing your bird in its cage. (If possible, bring your bird in its own cage. Leave the droppings and seed in the cage for examination but, of course, remove the water cup during transport.) Your doctor will observe the following:

- *Posture*—Fluffed and huddled? Position of wings? Does it perch properly? Are both legs and feet used normally? Is the bird crouched over its feet? Does the tail flick and flutter with each respiration?
- *Alertness*—Is the bird weak? Does it close its eyes as if it is sleepy? Is it wobbly? Is the bird interested in its surroundings?
- *Breathing*—What is its resting respiratory rate? Does the bird gasp and breathe with its mouth open?
- *Feathers*—Are the feathers ruffled? Are there broken or old feathers? Are there feathers on the cage bottom?
- *Droppings*—Are they well formed or watery? Normal color?
- *Seeds*—Are there hulls on the cage bottom or in the food cup (indicating that the bird is eating)?
- *Toys, perches, and covering*—Are they chewed? Kept clean? Are there any mites or lice?

Your doctor will restrain small birds (canaries, finches, budgerigars) with a bare hand and will probably use a towel or glove to hold the larger parrots. A good physical exam is very important. Do not talk to your doctor at this time unless a question is asked of you, since complete concentration is required.

The veterinarian will follow the same basic physical outlined in Chapter 2. The degree of pain, and the size, shape, or consistency of the tissues and organs will be determined by palpation and by using a stethoscope for *auscultation,* which allows the sounds of body functions (heartbeat, respiratory sounds) to be amplified. A visual inspection of your pet's perching, flight, posture, feathers, and other visible parts is also a part of a complete physical.

6. Does your veterinarian encourage you to ask questions?

All your questions should be answered in a clear, concise way and in language that you understand—not in medical jargon. Diagrams or simple line drawings are helpful, too.

7. Is your veterinarian gentle with your bird?

Sometimes a little calm talk and a quiet environment are all that is needed to make the exam easier.

8. Does your veterinarian own any pet birds?

9. Is your veterinarian careful with a biting or scratching bird?

Your veterinarian should explain that your bird will be gently but firmly restrained so that nobody gets hurt and so that your bird will not injure itself. Some doctors will use a veterinary assistant. Your doctor may request your assistance in placing the bird on the exam table.

10. **If you are a new bird owner, did the veterinarian provide literature on good health maintenance and training and explain the subject to you?**

11. **Will your doctor refer you to a veterinary specialist if needed?**

Good veterinarians know their limitations.

12. **Is your veterinarian a member of an emergency group, or is there another doctor on call when your veterinarian is not available?**

It is preferable for your doctor to leave the telephone numbers of other veterinarians who have a special interest in bird medicine.

13. **Are the rates and fees explained to you?**

A veterinarian's basic fees should *not* be based on the size of the animal or its original cost. The fee for an office visit will probably be the same for all pets—bird, dog, cat, or guinea pig. You are paying for professional advice based on many years of training and experience.

If your doctor does not offer the information, be sure to ask what the fees will be for the office exam, lab tests, radiographs, surgery, hospitalization, and treatment. Sometimes it is impossible to give you an exact figure, but high and low estimates are possible, unless the bird's condition is so unpredictable that the treatment may change. If your bird will be hospitalized for a few days, you could ask the doctor to keep you informed daily of your bird's accumulated tab. Many veterinary hospitals are nearly as well equipped as human hospitals, and the care should also be equivalent. Birds that need hospitalization frequently need close monitoring and special care. At the moment, though there is national pet care insurance for dogs and cats, there is none to take the sting out of paying the bills for birds' care, so knowing the daily financial picture as well as the health picture is important.

14. **Does your veterinarian use laboratory tests and radiographs (X-rays) discriminately to confirm a diagnosis?**

Your doctor should explain to you in simple language why each test or series of radiographs is being done. X-rays and other tests are often helpful in diagnosing illness and selecting the proper treatment.

15. **Does your veterinarian hospitalize only for serious problems?**

Hospitalization is not necessary in most cases. In fact, birds seem to fare better in their home environment, being treated by their owners in close cooperation with a veterinarian. Most treatment and lab tests can be done on an outpatient basis. Keep in mind that hospitalization can be expensive.

16. **Is your veterinarian's hospital well equipped?**

This may be difficult for you to evaluate, but up-to-date hospitals have modern radiograph equipment, surgical facilities, and laboratories.

The equipment that a veterinarian with a special interest in birds should have is discussed on pages 75–76.

If the answers to all these questions are positive, you have a wonderful veterinarian. If most of the answers are negative, or if you are not comfortable with your veterinarian's diagnosis or treatment, seek another doctor or another opinion.

A happy veterinarian-owner relationship also requires a cooperative, aware, and concerned owner. Even if you have the best of veterinarians, if you do not follow or understand instructions, your relationship—and your bird's health—can deteriorate rapidly. Because you live with your bird and know its habits and routine, you can often detect subtle changes that may go unnoticed by your doctor. The concerned and aware owner should use this book to best advantage by checking the appropriate Decision Charts and other sections whenever necessary.

When a visit is necessary, bring a notepad and write down (or have your veterinarian write down) *all* important instructions. Trying to remember everything is usually a waste of your time and money and may cause you to conclude mistakenly that a vet is incompetent. If you do not understand a medication—why it was prescribed, its side effects, or how long it should be given—or the importance, expectations, or limitations of a treatment or surgical procedure, ask your veterinarian to *make* it understandable. Lack of communication, not poor professional care, is the most frequent problem in the veterinarian-owner relationship.

For example, do *not* "double up" on the medication at night if you were too rushed in the morning to give your bird its medicine. Excess doses can be worse than none at all. Let your doctor demonstrate the best method to administer the medicine if you feel that you will have problems. And do *not* stop the medication just because your pet seems better. Follow your doctor's instructions. Stopping medication too early can cause an even more serious problem. If your bird experiences side effects from the medication, phone your veterinarian. A change in dosage or in the interval between doses—or a new drug altogether—may be recommended. If your doctor wants a follow-up exam, follow up!

One final word: Thank your doctor when he or she does a good job and is interested in your pet's health. Everyone, including your veterinarian, likes to be appreciated.

LABORATORY TESTS

Tests are often needed to confirm a diagnosis or to determine the best mode or the effectiveness of treatment. Some of the most common tests that may be requested are stool sample, skin scrapings, blood chemistry, bacteriology, and tissue biopsy.

Stool Sample

Intestinal parasites are not a common finding in pet birds, but tests for these should be done on a routine basis or when your bird is ill. A fresh sample from the cage floor should be adequate for examination. Also, see the information on giardia on page 68.

Tissue Scrapings

Confirming a yeast or fungus infection may involve transferring a tissue scraping of the lesion to a container that contains "fungus food." Confirmation may take one to two weeks. A direct slide can also be made to check for ringworm, candida, or aspergillosis. If there is a suspicion of a yeast or fungus infection, treatment will begin at the time of the scraping.

Blood Tests

The health of your bird's body depends on the health of all its parts, and an unhealthy organ will eventually affect the other organs. In order to confirm a diagnosis or to monitor your bird's return to health or its setbacks, various enzymes and products of metabolism found in the blood can be measured. An increase or decrease in their levels can be used to identify and monitor the organ or organs that are sick, and the proper treatment can be started. A blood test alone is *not* a substitute for a physical examination, but veterinary recognition of the importance of blood chemistries has made this commonplace for good veterinary care in dogs, cats, birds, and other companion animals.

Veterinarians are using reliable commercial laboratories or in-house blood analyzers that provide accurate results at a reasonable price on small amounts of blood. Blood samples can be collected safely and with little stress to your bird by cutting a toenail or an immature wing or tail feather. The right jugular vein, a leg vein, or a wing vein is used when larger amounts of blood are needed for blood tests. Your bird will be gently restrained as a small needle and syringe are used to collect the sample. Sometimes a bird is so sick or weak that testing should not be done until the bird is given intensive supportive care such as warmth and fluids.

Some helpful blood tests are as follows:

AST (SGOT) • High values (more than four times normal) may indicate liver disease.

Blood Sugar (Glucose) • Your doctor will run this test if diabetes is suspected.

Blood Uric Acid and Phosphorus • If kidney involvement from such problems as a tumor or gout is suspected, your doctor may run these tests.

Total Protein • This is a simple test to perform. Low values may reflect starvation, parasites, or chronic liver, intestinal, or kidney disease. A high value may indicate dehydration, shock, infection, or leukemia.

Other blood tests that may be helpful in diagnosis or prognosis are ones checking calcium, sodium, potassium, cholesterol, GGPT, and thyroid.

(White and red blood cell counts may indicate infection, parasitism, or anemia.)

Bone Marrow Aspiration or Biopsy

If the blood-forming cells need to be studied, bone marrow may be aspirated from the tibia (leg bone). Bone biopsies may be collected under anesthesia.

Fluorescent Antibody (FA) Tests

FA tests are being developed for the rapid diagnosis of Pacheco's disease, reovirus, papovavirus, and psittacosis.

Psittacosis Test

A psittacosis test should be included in the new-bird exam because parrot fever is contagious to other birds and humans. Any sleepy-eyed, poorly feathered, underweight bird with respiratory, digestive, or central nervous system signs may require a psittacosis test.

A blood test for antibody titers or a fecal culture for the psittacosis organism is useful. See "Psittacosis," page 69.

Urinalysis

If *diabetes mellitus* is suspected, the urine part of the droppings can be easily tested by a simple procedure called the *clinitest* exam for the presence of sugar. If there is sugar in the urine, a blood sugar test will be necessary to determine if your bird is a diabetic. The other parts of the urinalysis test that are commonly performed on our urine or that of dogs, cats, horses, or cows are also done on bird droppings.

Bacteriology

Bacterial infections are common in the pharynx, sinuses, and respiratory tract. Gram-negative bacteria are abnormal if cultured from the feces, throat, feather follicle, or internal organs of birds. Your doctor may suggest culture and sensitivity tests, which involve transferring a small amount of the infected material to a container filled with "food" in which the bacteria can flourish. Small paper disks, each containing a different antibiotic, are placed in the container at even intervals. The antibiotics that are effective against the bacteria will produce *zones of inhibition*—areas around the disks where no bacteria will grow. The bacteria will be identified by their growth pattern and microscopic features. Using a general antibiotic may cure an infection, but performing culture and sensitivity tests—especially in chronic infections—is better practice and may be cheaper in the long run.

Tissue Biopsy

Removing a section for microscopic examination is often an excellent way to make a proper diagnosis, determine if the disease process can be reversed, and select the best therapy. It is helpful in the diagnosis of external or internal tumors and in viral diseases such as bird pox. The biopsy is a good tool for determining the chances of your bird's recovery and the type and cost of the best therapy.

Radiographs (X–rays)

Since the laboratory tests for birds that are available to your doctor are limited, and since the anatomy of birds limits the ability to feel or hear all the organs during a physical exam, radiographs (X-rays) have become an important and helpful tool for diagnosing many illnesses in birds.

The radiographic equipment in many veterinary hospitals is equivalent to that in human hospitals—and just as expensive. Modern X-ray equipment provides excellent "pictures" of the bones and internal organs and the spaces between them. The process of taking X-rays is painless and relatively harmless. Sedation is only needed if your bird will not hold still. Any movement may cause blurring. Sedation should not be given if your bird is having breathing difficulty or is seriously ill. Two or more views are needed to get a three-dimensional "picture" of the area under investigation.

To get the "picture," X-rays are directed through your bird's body. They travel very rapidly and then penetrate a plate containing film. Thanks to the air sacs and hollow bones, bird X-rays show a nice contrast between the internal organs and the air-containing structures. X-rays pass through air easily, but solid masses, such as internal organs and bones, will stop some of them. Those rays hitting the film turn it black when it is developed. The areas on the film not touched by the rays remain white. So an X-ray has white areas (such as the heart, liver, and backbones) and black areas (lung tissue and air sacs). The doctor will study your bird's X-rays under a bright light, looking for changes in the normal shape, size, and density of the organs.

CAT (Computer Axial Tomography) scans may have value in the future in avian medicine. At present, such scans are experimental and very expensive.

Endoscopy

The endoscope allows your veterinarian to examine your bird's internal structures and organs. It is a fast, safe diagnostic procedure that allows direct observation.

A tube attached to a fiberoptic light source and lenses for magnification is inserted into the body. Small tweezers (forceps) can be attached to the end of the tube for taking tissue specimens for microscopic study and cultures.

Your doctor may find the endoscope helpful in the following situations:

- Checking for a foreign body (a seed, for example) that is suspected in the nostrils or trachea
- Investigating the sinuses
- Directly examining the crop for bacterial or fungal infections, or foreign bodies
- Examining the cloaca if there are signs of straining, bleeding, egg binding, or tissue protruding
- Exploring further if other tests are not conclusive with signs of vomiting, weight loss, abdominal swelling, feather picking, or paralysis of one leg
- Examining a bird that does not thrive or does not respond to conventional therapy
- Investigating signs of respiratory disease that persist despite normal X-rays
- Evaluating the gonads and internal organs of nonproductive breeding birds
- Surgically determining the sex

Laparoscopic examination (insertion of the endoscope into the abdomen) is generally not indicated in extremely weak or severely dehydrated birds. If a bleeding disorder is present, it should be corrected before laparoscopy. If there is a severe breathing problem, oxygen can be delivered through the trachea or the abdominal air sacs by way of a special tube. Surgical sexing is not recommended just to know if you have "a boy or girl"—only if you intend to breed.

Inhalation gas anesthesia (very safe) is indicated for laparoscopy.

Sexing

Blue-cered budgerigars are *usually* males. Some female cockatoo species have reddish-brown eyes. Cockatiels have their own distinctive sexual markings, but the sex of most parrot species can only be verified by surgical genetic or hormonal sexing—unless the bird lays an egg! (A female 100 percent of the time!)

Surgical sexing requires a laparoscopic examination. See "Endoscopy," page 85.

Genetic sexing analyzes the chromosomes of feathers, blood, or tissue cells. It will probably be available (as will hormone analysis) soon.

Cytology

The examination of cells in your bird's body can give your doctor a great deal of information. These cells can reflect the presence of bacterial, fungal, or psittacosis infection, malignancies, or inflammation.

The cells to be studied are collected in a variety of ways. For example, if your bird vomits frequently, aspirating crop contents with a soft plastic tube and studying the size, shape, and nature of the cells and fluid may help with diagnosis and treatment. A similar procedure can be used for sampling the sinuses and breathing tubes (trachea). In the near future, a bird may be sexed by cloaca cytology. Cytology smears of tissues and fluids are helpful when considered with other laboratory tests.

Electrocardiogram

The electrocardiogram (ECG) measures the electrical activity of the heart. The test causes no pain, but your bird has to lie still on a restraining board during the procedure. The electrocardiogram should be done if your bird has any of the following signs: coughing, shortness of breath, weakness, fainting, falling off the perch, or seizures. If your veterinarian hears a heart murmur or an abnormal rhythm, an ECG should be done. Infections or nutritional deficiencies can affect your bird's heart, so your doctor may do an ECG. Also, some medications can have a toxic side effect, and an ECG can pick up early heart changes. The ECG may be indicated before surgery and is useful in monitoring your bird under general anesthesia.

I would highly recommend that an ECG be included in the new-bird exam for the large parrots (Amazons, macaws, African greys, and cockatoos). The high purchase price, the stress of quarantine and domestication, and their longevity (60–70 years) warrant an ECG. It should also be part of the yearly "old-bird" exam.

Necropsy

This is the postmortem examination. An autopsy is helpful to your avian veterinarian if your bird dies. He or she learns from it so that other birds can be helped. It confirms or refutes what your doctor saw *clinically* in your bird, and the laboratory tests and radiographs (X-rays) will be compared to what your doctor observes during the autopsy. Tissues and cultures may be sent to the laboratory.

If your bird dies and you have other birds at home, the autopsy is recommended. If an infection or contagious disease is found, knowledge of the cause of death may save the lives of your other birds.

Anesthesia

Most owners are concerned about the risks of anesthetizing their bird. There are safe anesthetics that may be needed for many diagnostic and therapeutic procedures such as surgical sexing, diagnostic endoscopy, biopsy, radiology, fluid therapy, blood collection, blood transfusions, bandaging, and splinting.

You should be a good partner and well-informed consumer of veterinary care for your bird, so ask questions to ensure that *you* are comfortable with the anesthetic procedure and that your bird is a good candidate for anesthesia.

Ask the veterinarian the following questions:

Is anesthesia needed? If there will be pain or severe stress, it is required.

What type of anesthesia will be used? There are injectable and gas anesthetic agents. The safest are the inhaled agents such as isoflurane. The advantage of gas anesthesia is that the plane of anesthesia can be adjusted rapidly, and birds can be brought out of the anesthesia fast. It is even safe in critically ill patients.

Is my bird a good candidate for anesthesia? If your bird is anemic (pale); is in shock; or has fluid in the belly, breathing difficulties, severe weight loss, or dehydration, anesthesia is very risky but may be necessary to save your bird.

Are you and your staff experienced with bird anesthesia and handling of anesthetic emergencies?

Do you have recovery compartments? The recovery environment should be able to be maintained at ninety degrees Fahrenheit. You should be allowed to see not only the anesthesia equipment and how it works but also the recovery area. Is it kept clean and quiet? Are the birds watched *closely* during the recovery period?

Should my bird be fasted before anesthesia? A one- to three-hour fast is recommended. This will help prevent vomiting, regurgitation, and aspiration pneumonia. Intubating (placing a tube down the trachea) of the larger parrots will prevent aspiration pneumonia. Longer fasts may deplete your bird of needed sugar.

SURGERY

The most common pet avian surgeries are abdominal (foreign-body removals, tumors, egg peritonitis, biopsies, and exploratories), skin (wound repair, tumors, feather cysts), head and neck (mouth abscesses, sinuses), and fractures. Hysterectomies are done on birds that develop complications from egg laying (egg binding or egg peritonitis).

Avian surgery is a very state-of-the-art, delicate, and time-consuming field—in many cases, more involved than dog, cat, and even human pediatric surgery. A pediatric surgeon who once helped me remove a ten-gram tumor from the abdomen of a thirty-gram parakeet was amazed. His patients are usually thirty times larger than mine!

The Surgical Process

Bird surgery is much safer today, because your avian veterinarian will (1) evaluate and condition your bird before surgery, (2) monitor and support your bird during surgery, and (3) use special microsurgical instruments and monitor closely after surgery.

Evaluation

Your veterinarian will evaluate your bird by performing a complete physical examination and checking the weight. Other tests may be selected from this list: gram stain, culture and sensitivity, fecal, radiographs (X-rays), blood tests, and electrocardiogram. A good test is one of breathing recovery time. The breathing rate should return to normal within two minutes after handling.

Preconditioning

Preconditioning means getting your bird in the best shape possible before surgery. If a minor procedure is to be done on your healthy bird, minimal preconditioning is required. Chronic, debilitated states may necessitate antibiotics, fluid therapy, blood transfusions, warmth (in a hospital cage), and tube feeding.

Monitoring during Surgery

Your avian veterinarian and surgical staff will monitor body temperature, heart rate, blood pressure, and respiration during surgery. A special heating pad will keep your bird warm. Intravenous fluid may be administered. Blood for transfusions will be available.

Blood Transfusions

If your bird has severe bleeding from trauma or excessive hemorrhaging during surgery (for example, for the removal of a large tumor), a blood transfusion may be necessary. Avian veterinarians usually have a blood donor. Chicken, pigeon, or parrot blood can be administered to a parrot. Another transfusion cannot be given for a month without cross-matching. Cacul, my Amazon parrot, pays his room, board, and pizza bill by occasionally donating blood.

Microsurgery

An important advance in the field of bird surgery is the introduction of microsurgical techniques—a source of magnification such as an operating microscope; tiny, delicate surgical instruments; and electrosurgery. Since the surgical area is magnified, bleeding can be identified and stopped rapidly. Before such advances, hemorrhage was one of the major causes of surgical failure.

Monitoring after Surgery

Your veterinarian will carefully watch your bird after surgery and advise you on steps to take. During the healing period you should

- Be sure that your bird does not pick at the stitches. If it does, a protective collar may have to be put on its neck.
- Keep your bird warm and away from drafts.
- Do not let your bird fly free until the incision has healed.
- Keep toys and other cage furniture to a minimum so that the incision won't be irritated.
- Check your bird's food and water intake and its droppings daily.
- See "How Do I Know When My Bird Is Sick?," page 107 and the Decision Charts.

Wild bird rehabilitation is so advanced that repairing of the blood vessels, nerves, muscles, and tendons in bird bone fractures is now possible. However, just repairing the bone may not be adequate in getting birds of prey airborne again. The next major surgical breakthrough will be the repair and restoration of the joints. Dr. James E. Doyle, a Texas plastic surgeon with a special interest in hand surgery, has been a prime contributor to avian microsurgery. Such advances will speed the recovery of many ill and injured birds.

CHAPTER 5

Your Bird's Home Pharmacy

Your bird may sometimes require medication for minor illnesses and injuries. Many medical problems, such as minor abrasions or occasional loose droppings, resolve themselves without medication. A little time and knowledge are often all that are needed, and they may well be the most effective and least expensive treatment. This method should not be abused, however. If the Decision Charts recommend seeing a veterinarian or trying drug or nondrug treatments—such as cleaning and soaking a wound or withholding certain foods—follow the instructions carefully.

At the first sign of illness, be sure that your bird gets warmth, rest, and nutrition. Check the Decision Charts for the best way to help your bird get well.

BASIC NECESSITIES

A list of medications that are good to have on hand is presented here, as well as the ailments they treat. *Remember:* Keep all medicines out of the reach of children. The when and why of using medications, including dosage and side effects, are discussed afterward.

Medication	Ailment
Gevral Protein Mull-Soy Nutrical Gerber's High Protein baby food	Appetite loss
Monsel solution Styptic powder	Bleeding
Milk of magnesia Mineral oil	Constipation
Mineral oil	Crop impaction
Mineral oil	Egg binding
Antibiotic ophthalmic ointments	Eye irritations
Antibiotics	Bacterial infections (respiratory, digestive)
Kaopectate Pepto-Bismol	Loose droppings

Medication	Ailment
Hydrogen peroxide (3 percent) Activated charcoal Milk of magnesia	Poisoning • To induce vomiting • To absorb poison • To speed passage through the digestive tract
Kaopectate Pepto-Bismol	Regurgitation
Goodwinol Mineral oil Scalex Eurax	Scaly face, scaly leg
A and D Ointment Antibiotic ointment Aquasol A powder Domeboro solution Hydrogen peroxide (3 percent) Soap and water	Skin irritations
Lugol's iodine solution	Thyroid enlargement

Appetite Loss

It is a *very* serious matter when your bird stops eating. Food is needed to fuel its extremely high rate of metabolism and to maintain its normally high body temperature. You should see your veterinarian to find the cause of the problem. In many cases, force feeding and warmth should be used until the doctor can see your bird.

Gevral Protein

This is a therapeutic nutritional supplement that is used in human medicine. It is readily mixed with Mull-Soy and tube fed to birds that won't eat.

Dosage:
See "Tube Feeding" (page 100).

Mull-Soy

This is a hypoallergenic soybean formula that is used as a milk replacement for infants. It can be used as part of a mixture for tube feeding birds that won't eat. The approximate analysis is

Water	74 percent
Protein	6 percent
Fat	7.5 percent
Carbohydrate	11.0 percent
Calories	40 per fl. oz.

It also contains a good source of most essential vitamins and minerals. Since it contains too much water (it would cause diarrhea if given alone), it is usually thickened with equal parts of Gevral protein or Gerber's High Protein baby food for additional protein, vitamins, and minerals.

Dosage:
See "Tube Feeding" (page 100).

Nutrical

This is a high-calorie dietary supplement that can be purchased from your veterinarian. The supplement is mixed with an equal amount of warm water and tube fed to birds that are not eating.

Bacterial Infections

Antibiotics are only effective against *bacterial* infections and only if they are given in the proper dose for the proper length of time. Most over-the-counter antibiotics for birds are placed in the bird's water, but most birds don't drink much water. The best way to give antibiotics is directly into the bird's mouth or by injection. The over-the-counter drugs are worth a try, but keep in mind it may be better to see your veterinarian if you suspect that your bird has a bacterial infection.

Bleeding

Birds occasionally will break a nail or a young, growing feather, which may cause bleeding. If you trim a beak, nail, or young feather too short, bleeding may occur. Styptic powder, Monsel solution, or household flour are handy products to have available for such problems. Styptics can cause mouth burns, however, so be careful when using these near the beak.

Styptic Powder

Press some styptic powder into the bleeding area with a cotton-tipped applicator, clean cloth, or your finger. This should stop the bleeding immediately. Monsel solution can also be used to stop bleeding.

Constipation

This is a very *un*common problem in birds (see page 162).

Milk of Magnesia

The active ingredient, magnesium, causes fluid to be retained within the bowel and in the feces. It is also helpful in speeding passage of any poisons through the digestive tract.

Dosage:
Canaries, finches—1 drop in the mouth
Budgerigars, cockatiels and other small parrots—3-5 drops in the mouth
Large parrots—5-10 drops in the mouth

Side effects:
Milk of magnesia is nonabsorbable, but it does contain magnesium and some salt and should not be used for a prolonged time or if your bird has kidney or heart disease.

Mineral Oil

This is the cheapest and most effective laxative, but it can be dangerous if administered improperly or for a prolonged period. Mineral oil should be given in the mouth *very carefully* because it is bland and may enter the breathing tubes and lungs before your bird can cough. Mineral oil in the lungs will cause severe pneumonia. If mineral oil is given for a long period of time, it can cause deficiencies of the fat soluble vitamins A, D, E, and K.

Dosage (for two days at the maximum):
Canaries, finches—1 drop in the mouth
Budgerigars, cockatiels, and other small parrots—2-3 drops in the mouth
Large parrots—5-10 drops in the mouth

Side effects:
Pneumonia or vitamin deficiency if administered improperly.

Crop Impaction

Some birds will occasionally engorge themselves with grit. Giving mineral oil and massaging the crop are often helpful in breaking up the impaction.

Dosage and side effects:
Same as for constipation.

Egg Binding

Egg binding is sometimes cured with tincture of time, heat, and some warm mineral oil. *Note:* Egg binding is life threatening and needs immediate veterinary attention.

Dosage:
Same as for constipation, but it is administered into the other end—the vent (or cloaca)—with an eyedropper.

Eye Irritations

For short-term use, apply an opthalmic ointment (drops are preferable since they won't mat down the feathers) such as Neosporin or Neopolycin to your bird's eye two or three times daily. These ointments contain three antibiotics: polymycin, bacitracin, and neomycin.

Loose Droppings

If you have determined that the loose droppings are diarrhea, Kaopectate and Pepto-Bismol are safe medications for your bird. Do not use paregoric—it may be toxic. See your veterinarian if diarrhea persists or if the Decision Chart so indicates.

Kaopectate

Kaopectate contains *kaolin* and *pectin,* which coat the intestinal tract and help to form a solid stool.

Dosage:
Canaries, finches—1 drop in the mouth, 3 times daily
Budgerigars, cockatiels and other small parrots—2-3 drops in the mouth 3 times daily
Large parrots—5-10 drops in the mouth 3 times daily

Pepto-Bismol

Coats the intestinal tract and helps to form a solid stool.

Dosage:
Same as Kaopectate.

Poisoning

In case your bird ingests a poison, you need to have on hand hydrogen peroxide, activated charcoal, and milk of magnesia.

Hydrogen Peroxide

If your bird swallows a poison that can be expelled by vomiting, hydrogen peroxide 3 percent works very well. Do *not* induce vomiting if the poison swallowed is a petroleum-based compound or a strong acid or strong alkali (see "Poisoning," page 126). Be sure that the hydrogen peroxide purchased is not a higher strength (such as that used for bleaching hair).

Dosage:
Canaries, finches—1 drop in the mouth
Budgerigars, cockatiels, and other small parrots—2-3 drops in the mouth
Large parrots—5-10 drops in the mouth

If necessary, you can repeat this twice at 10-minute intervals until your bird vomits. If this treatment is unsuccessful, salt or a mustard–and–warm water solution can be put on the back of the tongue to induce vomiting.

Activated Charcoal

After your bird has vomited, you can administer a pinch (for small birds) to a quarter of a teaspoon (for large birds) of activated charcoal mixed in milk or water to absorb the poison if the specific antidote is not known. Activated charcoal can be purchased in drugstores.

Milk of Magnesia

To speed passage of the poison through your bird's digestive tract, use milk of magnesia.

Dosage:
Canaries, finches—1 drop in the mouth
Budgerigars, cockatiels, and other small parrots—2-3 drops in the mouth
Large parrots—5-10 drops in the mouth

Regurgitation

Kaopectate, Pepto-Bismol

These products soothe the crop, stomach, and intestinal lining.

Dosage:
Same as for loose droppings.

Scaly Face, Scaly Leg

Mineral oil or Scalex are two over-the-counter medications that may be helpful in cnemidocoptes infestations. Your veterinarian may prescribe medications that are more potent and effective.

Skin Irritations

Sterilizing Agents and Antiseptics

A little soap and water is the best way to clean a wound. Hydrogen peroxide (3 percent strength) cleanses wounds very well and is inexpensive. Betadine, a non-stinging iodine preparation, kills germs and is a good agent to use on the skin, but it is expensive.

Dosage:
Cleanse the wound three times daily. If necessary, pluck the feathers around the wound.

Domeboro Solution

This is a soothing wet dressing for relief of skin inflammation. It has antiseptic properties.

Dosage:
Dissolve one teaspoon or tablet in a pint of water. Apply wet dressings of the solution to the affected skin. You can repeat this twice daily.

Ointments and Creams

Oily medications must be applied carefully on birds. The feathers can become matted, and temperature regulation would be difficult. Only *small* areas should be treated with an ointment. A & D Ointment soothes irritated skin and can be applied twice daily to *small* affected areas. The ointments containing antibiotics (Neosporin, Neopolycin, and Mycitracin) can be applied to affected skin twice daily for no more than five days. Aquasol A cream soothes irritated skin very nicely and does not mat the feathers as much. It contains vitamin A in a water-miscible cream base and can be applied twice daily.

Powders

BFI powder is very good for skin irritations and wounds. It can be applied twice daily.

Thyroid Enlargement

An enlargement of the thyroid glands—called a goiter—is not uncommon in budgerigars. A diet of seeds deficient in iodine may cause such an enlargement of the thyroid glands, which press on the esophagus, and will result in regurgitation. Other symptoms include breathing difficulties (squeaking or wheezing with each breath), decreased appetite, and weight loss, as well as fluffing, huddling, and weakness.

Lugol's Iodine Solution

It is a good idea to keep budgerigars on a *preventive* dose so thyroid enlargement will not occur.

Preventive Dose:
Mix one-half teaspoon of Lugol's iodine solution with one ounce of water. One drop of this mixture can be placed in one ounce of drinking water *once* weekly. To *treat* thyroid enlargement (you may need a veterinarian's help for diagnosis), one drop of the mixture is mixed in one ounce of drinking water (for budgerigars), daily, for two weeks. *Note:* Lugol's iodine is *not* tincture of iodine (the solution that we use on our cuts and bruises).

THE HOME HOSPITAL

If your bird is ill and the Decision Charts recommend home treatment, or if you are not able to contact a veterinarian, set up your "home hospital." In fact, you should have the supplies for a home hospital handy and know when and how to use them—just in case—even when your bird is healthy.

Keep watch for *early* signs of illness in your bird. Some people say "when birds get sick, they just die." Well, this is because no home nursing care or veterinary attention is provided, or it is provided too late.

YOUR BIRD'S HOME HOSPITAL

Heat source—heating pad, radiator, 100-watt bulb or infrared lamp

Thermometer—to measure the home hospital temperature

Cage covering—towels or blanket

Half-inch adhesive tape or masking tape

Gauze bandages—half-inch rolls

Sterile gauze pads

Cotton-tipped swabs (Q-tips)

Rubbing alcohol

Tweezers

Sharp scissors with rounded ends

Plastic medicine dropper

Feeding tubes and syringes—obtained from and demonstrated by your veterinarian

Mull-Soy, Gevral, Gerber's High Protein baby food, Nutrical—alternate food sources if your bird is not eating and tube feeding is necessary.

Plastic medicine dropper

Vaporizer—to be used after instructions from your veterinarian

Medications (see "Basic Necessities," pages 91–92)

At the first sign of illness, check the Decision Charts to see if home treatment is advised. If so, the important things to provide are *warmth, rest, food, water,* and possibly some *medication.* A bird must eat to maintain its high metabolic rate to keep up its high body temperature. If your bird is sick, you want to provide food that will be easily digested. (You don't want your bird to use up its energy trying to digest foods.)

Warmth

All sick birds benefit from warmth. The home hospital cage should be kept between eighty-five to ninety degrees Fahrenheit. The heat source can be a heating pad set on "low" under the cage (be sure it can't be chewed), or a 100-watt bulb or infrared lamp placed near the cage. A sheet or towel should cover most—but not all—of the cage (your bird needs ventilation). Monitor the cage temperature with a thermometer placed near the outside of the cage. Placing the cage near a radiator provides a less desirable heat source.

Many sick birds respond (by becoming more active) when given this extra heat. If they become overheated, they will pant and hold their feathers tightly against their body. If they become chilled, they will be inactive and fluffed-up.

Rest

Be sure that a sick bird is given twelve hours of darkness each day and no noise. Stress-free rest allows the bird to conserve its energy and fight off viruses, bacteria, and other "bad guys."

Food

Remove the grit. Sick birds will sometimes gorge themselves with grit.

If your bird is still eating but showing less interest in food, try to arouse its appetite. Stir the food and put it on the cage floor (this is not hygienic, but your bird may not have the energy or interest to perch); provide privacy, and remove the perches; provide a variety of fresh foods (seeds, greens, fruit, baby food, cereal, cooked egg yolk, pound cake, crackers, dry dog or cat food, etc.); soak the seeds (this may make them easier for your bird to eat).

Force feeding will be necessary if your bird won't eat. If you find your bird on the bottom of the cage—a "down bird"—*gently* pick it up and feed it some quick energy with a dropper: honey-and-water solution, Gatorade, or orange juice may get it on its feet temporarily. This dose may have to be repeated every fifteen minutes for a few times. The total amount may be

Finches and canaries—7 drops
Cockatiels—1–2 teaspoons
Amazons—1–3 teaspoons
Cockatoos—5–8 teaspoons

Dropper Feeding

You can try dropper feeding a sick bird egg yolk and milk. This is only a temporary measure until you can see a doctor or until tube feeding can be started. A vitamin-mineral supplement should also be added.

Tube Feeding

Tube feeding is a very effective method for providing much-needed nutrition to your bird if it won't eat. The necessary equipment can be provided by your veterinarian, and after a demonstration, you may be able to help nurse your bird at home upon your veterinarian's recommendation. *Note:* Tubing an extremely sick bird, especially one with breathing problems, may make matters worse, so *always* consult your veterinarian before tube feeding. You will need a plastic syringe and a piece of plastic or rubber tubing. The diameter of the tubes is indicated by the notation "F" (French):

Tube Size

Finches and canaries—use 5F tube
Budgerigars, cockatiels, or lovebirds—use 8F or 10F tube
Larger parrots—use 15F tube

Formulas

Many different formulas work well. A few that you may like to try are

1. Gerber's High Protein baby food mixed in warm water, Soylac or Mull-Soy. You can also add a little egg yolk, baby food, and a vitamin-mineral supplement.
2. Gevral Protein (one part) to Mull-Soy (three parts)
3. Peanut butter (smooth) with corn oil. Add a little egg yolk, baby food, and a vitamin-mineral supplement.

The following amounts can be fed to your bird two or three times daily. (Be sure to provide your bird with its daily water needs also.)

Canaries—¼ to ½ ml.
Budgerigars—1 to 2 ml.
Cockatiels—2 to 4 ml.
Amazons—15 to 20 ml.
Macaws—15 to 30 ml.
Cockatoos— 20 to 40 ml.

The Technique

Small birds such as finches, canaries, budgerigars, and cockatiels can be held in the palm of the hand with the forefinger in back of the head, the thumb under the jaw, and other fingers loosely holding the wings and feet. *Do not put pressure on the chest.* Your bird breathes by expanding its chest. A bird sick enough to be tube fed usually won't struggle—so be very gentle. At the first sign of distress, *stop*—then return the bird to its cage to rest.

Larger parrots can be gently wrapped in a towel, with the head held firmly. A speculum to keep the mouth open (which can be provided by your veterinarian) may be needed.

The tube must be placed in the mouth, down the esophagus, and into the crop (see Chapter 2 for information on the location of these structures). Your bird's head must be *extended away* from the body in order to pass the tube down the esophagus. Measure the distance from the tip of the beak to the bottom of the neck with a felt-tip marker on the tube.

Insert the feeding tube at the side of the beak (most birds can't break the tube

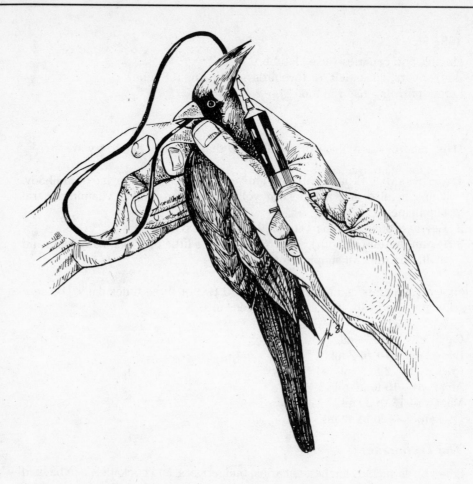

with the side of their beak), and slide it gently down into the crop. You can often see the tube passing down the neck. If the tube doesn't go down easily, stop. Pull it out and moisten with formula and reinsert it. The back of the throat, esophagus, and crop tissue can be punctured if you are not gentle or try to force the tube. In larger parrots, check to see that the tube is in the back of the throat and not in the "breathing hole" (unlikely, but possible). When the "tip of the beak" mark is reached, the tube is in the crop. Gently and slowly begin to feed the formula.

Administer a small amount of formula at first. If formula appears at the mouth, remove the tube and tilt the head downward so that the bird won't choke on the formula. Some birds are so weak that their crop loses its strength and regurgitation occurs. In these cases, the tube must be passed to the stomach. This should be done by your veterinarian. *Note:* Be slow in rotating a sick bird; you may cause it to go into irreversible shock.

After giving the formula, remove the tube and hold the bird for a minute or two. Talk to it to distract it so that it won't regurgitate. After placing your bird back in its cage, watch it and talk to it for a few minutes.

Be sure to use fresh formula for each feeding. Clean the tube and syringe thoroughly and let them air-dry on a paper towel.

Other Hints

- Be sure to feed your bird a vitamin-mineral supplement.
- Check the amount and character of your bird's droppings. Keep a chart. Put waxed paper or plastic wrap on the cage bottom.
- Try to tempt your bird with different types of food.
- *The home hospital should be run with your veterinarian as your partner. Keep in touch with him or her.*

PART II

Caring
for Your
Bird

HOW TO USE THIS SECTION

Most of the problems common to birds are described in this section. Many of them can be treated at home without visiting your veterinarian. The Decision Charts will help you become confident in diagnosing problems and finding the right treatment for your bird. Prevention is also discussed. Remember the old adage, "An ounce of prevention is worth a pound of cure."

Finding the Right Decision Chart

If you suspect an illness, determine the chief sign—for example, cere problems—and look it up in the contents or index to find the page where the subject is discussed. If your bird has more than one problem simultaneously, you may have to use more than one Decision Chart. For instance, if your pet has cere problems and decreased appetite, check the chart for each problem. If one recommends home treatment and the other advises a visit to your veterinarian, *see your veterinarian.*

Using the Decision Charts

It is very important to read all the general information on a particular problem. In many cases, the chart may advise you to see the doctor immediately, but emergency treatment may also be needed before you get to the doctor's office. After reading the information, start at the top of the Decision Chart (do not skip around) and answer each question.

If home treatment is indicated, follow all instructions exactly, or the treatment will not be effective. If your bird is not improving, even with good care, *see your veterinarian.*

If the chart indicates veterinary consultation, it does not necessarily mean that the illness is serious. It may mean that more vigorous treatment or further examination and lab tests are needed. "See veterinarian NOW" means *immediate attention is needed;* "See veterinarian within 24 hours" means attention is needed but not immediately; "Make appointment with veterinarian" means a visit should be made within a few days.

The procedures discussed in the next section will give you step-by-step guidance on how to handle any emergency. Read the entire section and practice the procedures to become familiar with them *before* you have to use them. Your veterinarian will be happy to help you with any you don't fully understand. I hope you'll never have to use these procedures, but your doctor will be very proud of you for being a prepared and a helpful partner if an emergency does occur.

Chapters 6 and 7 will help you recognize an emergency situation. Your job is to preserve your bird's life and to prevent injury until veterinary care is available. *Note:* There are some other emergencies listed in Chapter 8, so become familiar with the situations described in that chapter as well. In addition, certain problems require emergency treatment from you before going to the doctor's office, so read the descriptive sections carefully *before* an emergency develops.

HOW DO I KNOW WHEN MY BIRD IS SICK?

You usually know all the symptoms when your dog or one of your children is not feeling well. But what about when your bird isn't? Your bird's cough may be only a subtle clicking sound, and diarrhea may be just some loose droppings on the cage paper—but these may be serious problems to your bird. In order to be aware of any illness in your bird *early,* become familiar with the following signs:

- Your bird's behavior changes; it becomes sleepy (eyes closing), less active, and withdrawn.
- There is a change in appetite. Loss of appetite (*anorexia*) or increased appetite (*polyphagia*) may indicate illness.
- Your bird drinks more water than normal.
- Droppings become loose or change color.
- The *number* of droppings decreases. Count the number of droppings *daily* when changing the cage. Fewer droppings may indicate that your bird is not eating well, the first and most subtle sign of many illnesses.
- Your bird "fluffs up" (a sign of a chilled and hungry bird).
- A long molt and scratching or picking of feathers occur.
- A change in or loss of voice or song is apparent.
- Sneezing, clicking respiration (cough), brown-stained feathers above the nostrils (runny nose), or breathing difficulty occurs.
- Tail bobbing, sitting "down on the perch" (crouching over its feet), and sitting on the floor of the cage can be serious signs of illness.

6

Emergency Procedures

APPROACHING AN INJURED BIRD

If injured, even the friendliest bird may try to bite because of fear and pain. Furthermore, an injured bird that is frightened may injure itself further. Approach the bird *slowly,* talking in a quiet and reassuring voice. Bend down *slowly* to the bird's level, still talking calmly.

RESTRAINT

The least amount of handling (and the gentlest) is the best restraint for an ill or injured bird. Careless handling may cause irreversible shock or death. Small birds such as canaries, finches, and budgerigars can be held with the bare hand. *Remember:* A bird's breastbone must go up and down when it breathes. So hold a bird only on its sides or you will suffocate it.

Small birds will rest comfortably in the palm of your hand, with the head and neck held between the thumb and forefinger. Large birds such as cockatiels, conures, and other parrots, and macaws and cockatoos can be wrapped in a thin, folded towel. Restrain the head and neck with one hand and the body and wings with the other. Here's a little trick that will help you get an obstinate large bird out of its cage: As it climbs up the bars, hold one of its legs. When it grasps the bar with its beak, quickly grab its head and neck. Remember, large birds may bite! So be gentle and cautious as you handle *any* bird.

TREATING SHOCK

Shock is caused by severe insult to your bird's body—bleeding, trauma, fear, fluid loss (for example, from loose droppings), infection, heart failure, or breathing problems. It is a syndrome in which the heart and blood vessels are unable to deliver the nutrients and oxygen to the cells and are equally unable to remove the toxic waste products from the cells. If the shock process is not treated promptly, it may be impossible to reverse and your bird may die.

There are several major signs of shock in humans, dogs, and cats: pale or muddy gums; a weak or rapid pulse; capillary refilling that takes longer than two seconds; rapid breathing; a low rectal temperature, with skin and legs cool to the touch; and weakness or unconsciousness. Of course, it is difficult to determine most such signs in your bird.

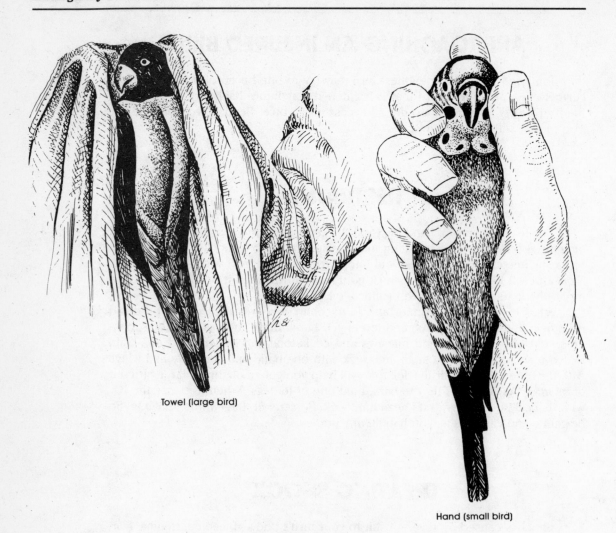

Towel (large bird)

Hand (small bird)

Restraint Techniques

If your bird shows any of the following signs, assume that it is probably in shock—whatever the cause.

1. Weakness
2. Fluffing up
3. Heavy breathing

Maintaining body heat and transporting your bird very gently to your veterinarian's office are the two most helpful things that you can do. If possible, phone the hospital so that they can prepare for your bird.

Your veterinarian will try to maintain your bird's body temperature with an incubator or heat lamp. Oxygen, fluids, and *corticosteroids* may be given. Corticosteroids, which are hormones produced by the adrenal gland, have many functions, one of which is to help cells fight destructive agents. They are also produced synthetically by pharmaceutical companies for use in human as well as veterinary medicine. In shock, the capillaries are like a dry riverbed. Fluids flood the capillaries and renew the vigorous blood flow that nourishes the "dried-out" cells.

Do not handle your sick or injured bird excessively, and do not change its position rapidly. For example, a budgerigar should be moved *slowly* from a horizontal to a vertical position while being held in your hand. A fast lift or rotation can cause shock to progress to the irreversible stage.

TREATING OILY BIRDS

Birds can lose their insulation when their feathers are soaked with oil. If they swallow oil, loss of appetite, anemia, and damage to the intestines, eyes, and kidneys can occur as well.

These are the recommended steps to cleaning a bird that has been covered with oil in an emergency.

1. Warm the bird.
2. Bathe the bird in a solution of one part mild detergent, such as Lux or Dawn, and nine parts water warmed to about 104° F. Stroke the feathers in the direction of their growth. Rinse and repeat the strokes until the water beads off the feathers (usually 4–5 times).
3. Fluids and force feeding may be necessary.
4. Place opthalmic ointment in the bird's eyes.
5. Wrap the bird in a diaper to prevent it from preening and to help keep it warm.

Of course, this procedure is best done by trained people: avian veterinarians and bird rescue personnel. If you can get to an avian hospital, call them to say that you are coming. Keep your bird warm, and go to the hospital immediately.

TRANSPORTING THE ILL OR INJURED BIRD

Warmth and *gentleness* are the key points to remember when transporting an ill or injured bird—a bird that will be having a difficult time maintaining its normal body temperature. The following procedures are important:

1. The bird should be brought to the hospital in its *own* cage—not in a shoe box or pillowcase.
2. Remove water cup, perches, and toys from the cage.
3. Leave all droppings in the cage so that your doctor can examine them.
4. Cover the cage with a blanket—to keep your bird warm and to reduce the stress of unfamiliar noises and sights.
5. If it is a cold day, warm up the car before putting the bird in.
6. Be sure that your bird is transported gently. Do not change its position rapidly.
7. Bring along any medicine that your bird has been taking.

The same procedures should be followed with ill or injured wild birds, although a box (with air holes) or some other makeshift holding cage may have to be used to transport the bird to your veterinarian's office.

Accidents and Injuries

BLEEDING, CUTS, AND WOUNDS

Cage and aviary birds may get cuts and wounds from fighting, scratching, or chewing on themselves or from sharp projections (wire, damaged toys). Wild birds frequently sustain wounds from struggling to escape hungry cats, fighting with other birds, flying into wires or windows, or being shot (by BBs or pellets).

If there is severe external or internal bleeding (in small birds that may be only a few drops) or a puncture wound in the crop, lungs, air sacs, abdomen, or eye, quick supportive care is important. The bird will be short of breath and weak, and it may collapse.

In such cases, you must stop the bleeding, provide warmth, and transport your bird *gently* to the veterinarian's office.

Bleeding can also be caused by a calcium or vitamin K deficiency (especially in conures). Inflammation of the intestine or cloaca, toxins, liver disease, or a bleeding cheesy mass in the mouth (usually caused by a vitamin A deficiency) may be sources of bleeding.

Home Treatment

If a skin wound is not too deep (and does not involve important structures or organs), not too long, and not too wide, it will heal nicely in most cases. Clean the wound with soap and warm water after the bleeding stops. Hydrogen peroxide (3 percent) can also be used. Be gentle. If you rub the wound too hard, the clot may loosen and the bleeding will recur. Using tweezers, gently remove any feathers, dirt, or other foreign material from the wound. Clean the wound daily and apply a topical antibiotic cream or powder.

Nails or feathers sometimes bleed if they are broken or cut too short. Direct pressure or a styptic pencil or powder can be used to help stop the bleeding. Always pull the feather out if it is bleeding.

A puncture injury in the neck area can damage the crop wall. Food and liquids will pass out the hole in the neck. If a doctor is not available and the bird is stabilized—breathing well, alert, and active—you can suture the crop area so that the bird can eat; otherwise, death will occur from starvation and dehydration.

You will need a pair of scissors, tweezers, a sewing needle, and thread. Soak all items in alcohol. Pluck feathers around the wound. Clean the wound with soap and warm water, then rinse it with 3 percent hydrogen peroxide. Using the tweezers, pick up the underlying tissue and skin, and hold it taut while you push the needle and thread through. Tie each stitch separately. Although the bird will probably feel some pain during this procedure, the crop must be closed if the bird is to survive. A soft-food diet of milk-soaked bread, hard-boiled eggs, and fruit should be fed for a few days.

What to Expect at the Veterinarian's Office

If your bird is "shocky," warmth and other supportive care will be provided. Paralysis of the wings and/or legs may indicate brain or spinal cord injury. Weakness, breathing difficulties, or unconsciousness, of course, indicates serious injury.

If there is a puncture wound in the crop, chest, or abdomen, surgery may be required. Your doctor may feel that the wound needs no sutures, just flushing with warm sterile water and a topical antibiotic. Open wounds heal by skin contraction and by the presence of serum and blood cells at the site. Even gap-

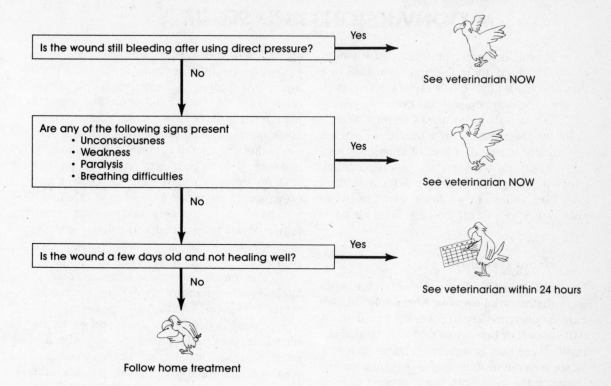

Is the wound still bleeding after using direct pressure?

Yes → See veterinarian NOW

No ↓

Are any of the following signs present
- Unconsciousness
- Weakness
- Paralysis
- Breathing difficulties

Yes → See veterinarian NOW

No ↓

Is the wound a few days old and not healing well?

Yes → See veterinarian within 24 hours

No ↓

Follow home treatment

ing wounds will heal in time by this process if kept clean. Hospitalization, warmth, fluids, blood transfusions, and other medications may be necessary. Blood tests, cultures, and endoscopy may be done after stabilization.

CONVULSIONS AND SEIZURES

Convulsions are temporary disturbances of electrical activity in the brain that lead to a loss of control of all bird's skeletal muscles. A severe or lengthy convulsion does not necessarily indicate the presence of serious disease or injury. The signs of a generalized seizure are an inability to stand, a loss of consciousness, and violent muscle spasms (legs twitching, wings flapping, and shaking). After a seizure, your bird will seem confused and unresponsive. It may just sit on the cage floor for a few hours.

Home Treatment

EMERGENCY—Clear the area of any objects that may injure your bird while the seizure is occurring. Try to cover your bird gently with a towel or blanket so that it will not injure itself. There may be several seizures in a row. When the convulsions stop, calmly and quietly reassure the bird with your presence. Keep lights and noise to a minimum. Provide warmth (if the seizure is not caused by heat stroke), and use a dropper to give your bird a sugar-water solution or warm water and honey when it can swallow. Be gentle and stop if your bird struggles. Seek veterinary aid as soon as you can.

What to Expect at the Veterinarian's Office

Your veterinarian will perform a complete physical examination and blood tests and may suggest hospitalization. A psittacosis test may be done. X-rays will be taken if lead poisoning is suspected. (Lead will show up on X-rays.) An electrocardiogram will be done if heart disease is suspected. In veterinary medicine, a good history is very important for diagnosis. Did your bird fly into an object (head injury) or become severely frightened (head injury or "capture" syndrome)? Has it shown other signs of illness? Did your bird ingest a plant, chemical, or heavy metal poison? Did it chew on paint (lead poisoning)? What is your bird's diet (B vitamin or protein deficiency, or bad seed)? Was your bird in direct sunlight with no shade provided (heat stroke)? African grey parrots are prone to low blood calcium. If you have an African grey, talk to your veterinarian about proper diet and calcium supplements. Red lored amazons, mynahs, and peach-faced lovebirds are prone to epilepsy.

The most common causes of convulsions are head injury, infections (bacterial, viral, or fungal), psittacosis, poisons, "epilepsy," vitamin deficiency, low blood sugar, low blood calcium, kidney disease, liver disease, heart disease, heatstroke, "stroke" (old parrots), and enlarged thyroid (budgerigars). Regardless of the cause, warmth (except for heatstroke) and other supportive therapy such as nutrition and possibly fluids are necessary. Your doctor may prescribe the following treatments if the cause can be determined: *Head injury or "capture syndrome"* (corticosteroids—to decrease brain swelling and to help stop hemorrhage); *bacterial infection* (antibiotics); *"epilepsy"* (anticonvulsants); *vitamin deficiency* (B vitamin injections and a balanced diet); *low blood sugar or calcium* (sugar or calcium solution); *enlarged thyroid* (iodine solution and thyroid medication).

Prevention

Cover mirrors and windows to avoid *head* injury during flight time. Read about poisoning later in this chapter. To avoid *bacterial*

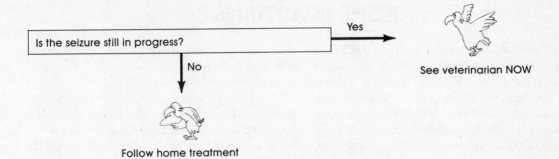

Is the seizure still in progress?

Yes → See veterinarian NOW

No ↓ Follow home treatment

infections, wash your hands before handling your bird or its food. Maintain your bird on a varied and well-balanced diet. To avoid thyroid enlargement in budgerigars, use a maintenance dose of Lugol's iodine solution in the drinking water (see page 98). Do not let your bird chew on lead-based paint or anything containing lead. Do not use cooking utensils or range drip pans coated with *polytetra fluoroethylene* (nonstick surfaces such as Teflon or Silverstone) around your bird. If these are overheated, the toxic fumes cause respiratory distress, incoordination, seizures, and rapid death.

BONE FRACTURES

Your bird may have a fracture if it (1) is not bearing weight on a leg, (2) has a crooked leg or wing, (3) has leg pain (holding leg up) and swelling, or (4) has a drooping wing. *Crepitus,* the sound or feel of bone rubbing on bone, is even stronger evidence of a fracture. If a piece of bone is protruding through the skin, there is no doubt.

In a *compound* fracture, a bone fragment penetrates the surface, and severe damage to the skin, muscle, nerves, and blood vessels can result. Delayed healing and infections can be serious problems in compound fractures since bone is not very resistant to infection. Birds have many hollow bones; therefore, infections can spread through the compound fracture site to the air sacs and lungs if the wound is not cleaned and covered soon.

Concussions and fractures of the vertebrae are common in wild birds. You will see a paralysis of both legs and possibly a weakness or fluttering of the wings. These birds usually die quickly of respiratory paralysis.

Home Treatment

It is important to immobilize the fracture site and the bird until you or your veterinarian can splint the leg or wing. A bird with a fracture is undergoing stress, so the usual supportive measures are recommended. Here are some tips if you want to splint the fracture yourself (when in doubt, consult your veterinarian).

The most frequently fractured leg bones are the tibiotarsus and the tarsometatarsus. The best restraint for splinting is to place a small bird in a sock or the foot of a stocking for restraint. A larger bird can be restrained in a thin towel, with its head protruding.

Gently pull the leg and press on the fracture site to appose the break (traction). Place three layers of adhesive tape over the fracture site, and then press together at the front and back of the leg.

Masking tape or adhesive tape can be used for wing fractures. Place the tip of the fractured wing on the tip of the normal wing. Wrap a strip of tape around the body, including the wings. Leave the end of the tape loose for the moment. Place a second strip of tape down the back, including the wings, then fold this strip under the wing tips. Fold over the loose end of the first strip. Place a counterbalance strip around the body and wing tips (do not include the cloaca) so that the bird can keep its balance.

Technique for Taping Fractured Wing

Left side view

Right side view

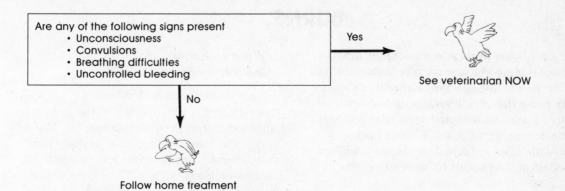

Are any of the following signs present
- Unconsciousness
- Convulsions
- Breathing difficulties
- Uncontrolled bleeding

Yes → See veterinarian NOW

No ↓ Follow home treatment

Compound fractures must be cleaned well with peroxide, alcohol, or medicated soap. Dirt and broken feathers must be removed from the wound. An antibiotic ointment should be used and the skin sutured before the splint is applied.

A bone fracture should heal well within four weeks if the broken bones are in good alignment, if there is no infection, and if your bird does not peck off the splint.

Don't be hasty in splinting a bird's leg unless it is obviously crooked or the bone is protruding. Even waiting a day may surprise you. Sprains are easily mistaken for breaks, and your bird may be walking on that "broken" leg the next day!

Before you splint a leg that is *not* broken, see "Lameness" (page 119) and "Nail and Toe Troubles" (page 174).

What to Expect at the Veterinarian's Office

Your veterinarian will check all systems to make sure that they were not damaged when your bird was injured, and to ascertain that the problem is a fracture and not some other lameness or foot or toe trouble.

A radiograph (X-ray) may be needed to verify the fracture and to determine the best method of repair. Most bird fractures heal with external stabilization (splints), but some larger birds may need internal fixation (metal pins, plates, or wires) for proper healing. Some injured limbs, especially wings, will not heal with good functional range of motion without special microsurgery. This specialized surgery attempts to repair blood vessels, nerves, muscles, tendons, and joints. Discuss the chances of healing and the cost of each technique with your veterinarian. Today, no bird has to be put to sleep because it has a fracture—a crooked-legged bird is still more agile and can still perch better than a two-legged person!

Prevention

Be sure that the cage is in a safe place where it cannot be tipped over. When your bird has flight time around the room, cover mirrors and windows, and be sure that pets not socialized to the bird are not present. Keep toenails trimmed so that they do not get caught in things. Cage only compatible birds together. Be careful when cleaning the cage—don't catch the bird's leg in the cage pan. Don't buy any toys that can trap wings or legs and don't clutter the cage with toys.

BURNS

Free-flying birds may sometimes mistake a pot of boiling chicken soup or a hot burner for an interesting landing strip. If it's your bird's lucky day, it will swoop up fast and just lightly "toast" its feet and legs. The feathers fortunately protect the rest of your bird.

With skin reddened, your bird will be fluffed up and reluctant to move or perch.

Home Treatment

EMERGENCY—Flush the feet and legs with cold water. Gently dry the area with clean or sterile gauze. You can also apply cold compresses. An antibiotic cream can be used. Deep or extensive burns should be seen by your veterinarian immediately. Treatment for shock may be required.

For chemical burns, flush with cold water until all traces of the chemical are gone. Treat for shock.

What to Expect at the Veterinarian's Office

Your veterinarian will determine the severity of the burns. Cleaning the burns and giving antibiotics may be all that is needed. More serious burns may require force feeding, fluid therapy, steroids, antibiotics, and warmth in the incubator. Hospitalization is also necessary for such cases since close nursing care may be the only way to save your bird's life. Sometimes toes will have to be amputated or they may slough. Your bird can still lead a normal life without some toes and even without a leg.

Prevention

If free-flight time cannot be restricted to non-cooking hours, keep your exercising bird out of the kitchen or cover boiling liquids. Chicken soup is supposed to have healing qualities, but "parboiled parrot" will not improve the soup.

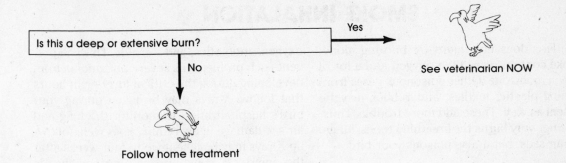

Is this a deep or extensive burn? —— Yes ——> See veterinarian NOW

No

Follow home treatment

SMOKE INHALATION

Fire does not injure by burning alone: Smoke contains very little oxygen and a lot of carbon monoxide. Other poisonous gases from burning plastic, textiles, and rubber may be present as well. These add more trouble. Thus, a fire not only burns the breathing tubes, lungs, and air sacs, but it also poisons your bird.

Home Treatment

EMERGENCY—Remove your bird to fresh air. Treat your bird for shock, then seek the aid of a veterinarian.

What to Expect at the Veterinarian's Office

If your bird is conscious, and there is no blood-tinged material being coughed up and no fluid in the lungs or air sacs, it may be placed in an incubator and given humidified oxygen, antibiotics, and steroids. This will prevent such problems as severe pneumonia from developing during the critical forty-eight hours that follow. X-rays may be taken during your bird's hospitalization to monitor the lung and air sac damage. If everything goes well, follow-up X-rays may be taken two to four weeks after the injury. If your bird is unconscious, is coughing up blood-tinged material, or has pneumonia, the outlook is more serious.

Prevention

Smoke alarms should be installed, and other fire prevention measures should be taken. Your local fire department or humane shelter can provide you with a decal to place on your front door that will inform the fire department of the number of pets to look for and their usual location in your home in case of fire.

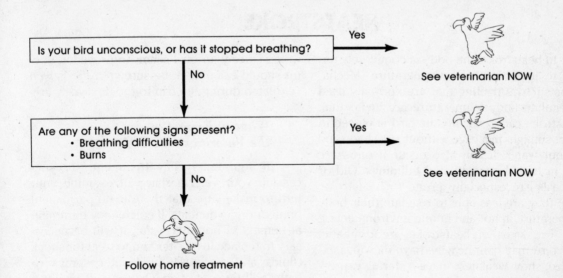

Is your bird unconscious, or has it stopped breathing? **Yes** → See veterinarian NOW

No ↓

Are any of the following signs present?
- Breathing difficulties
- Burns

Yes → See veterinarian NOW

No ↓

Follow home treatment

HEATSTROKE

In heatstroke, the body is completely unable to lower its body temperature. Mechanisms such as panting that are normally used to regulate body temperature are ineffectual. Heatstroke can occur if your bird is placed in direct sunlight in a cage without any shade and without water. It can also occur if birds are kept in humid, unventilated buildings. Old or fat birds are especially prone to heatstroke, since they are less able to regulate their body temperature in hot and humid environments.

The signs of heatstroke are dramatic. Your bird may pant heavily, have its wings extended, show weakness, have a staring expression, and collapse.

Home Treatment

EMERGENCY—A high body temperature must be lowered rapidly to avoid brain damage or death. A cold-water spray or bath must be given immediately. Being taken to an air-conditioned room also helps bring the fever down. If your bird stops panting, seems more relaxed, and responds normally to your voice, it is doing well. Give your bird a small amount of water. Once your bird seems improved, a doctor should examine it. Be sure your car is well ventilated during the trip to the doctor.

What to Expect at the Veterinarian's Office

If your emergency treatment was successful, your veterinarian will examine your bird to make sure that there is no permanent brain or organ damage. If emergency treatment at home was not successful, it will be necessary to replace lost water and to treat for shock (fluids and steroids). Cold-water sprays or baths will be continued. Oxygen will be given if needed, and your bird may be hospitalized so that it can be observed closely for twenty-four hours.

Prevention

Adequate ventilation, shade, and free access to water are necessary. If you place your caged bird near a window, remember that the sun changes direction and that your bird can get overheated if no shade is available.

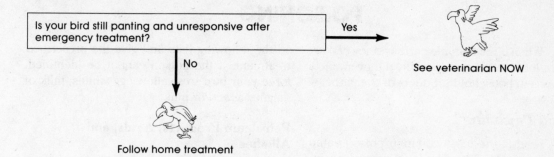

Is your bird still panting and unresponsive after emergency treatment?

Yes → See veterinarian NOW

No ↓

Follow home treatment

POISONING

When birds become curious, they can get into a lot of trouble—especially if they swallow poisons in household products or the garbage.

Lead Poisoning

Lead is the most common poison eaten by caged and wild birds. Sources of lead include: antiques; lead frames of stained-glass windows; Tiffany lamps; weighted items (ash trays, plastic toy penguins); fishing, scuba, and drapery weights; the foil from champagne and wine bottles; batteries; solder; bullets and air-rifle pellets; old paint; sheetrock; galvanized chicken wire; linoleum; mirror backing; light-bulbs bases; dolomite and bone meal products; and leaded gasoline fumes.

The clinical signs are sleepiness, weakness, green or black diarrhea, bloody feces (Amazons), regurgitation and central nervous system signs (wing droop, head tilt, or seizures). It is treatable if recognized early.

Diagnosis is by radiographs (X-rays). The dense lead particles will be seen. A blood test for lead is also helpful.

Calcium EDTA injection is the treatment of choice.

Home Treatment

EMERGENCY—If your bird has swallowed a poison, call your poison control center immediately and get veterinary aid. Two animal poison control hotlines are, in Georgia, (404) 542-6751, and in Illinois, (217) 333-3611.

Take a container with the poison and a sample of the regurgitation to the veterinarian. If your bird stops breathing, give artificial respiration. If you cannot reach your veterinarian or poison control center, check for the poison on the following lists and give the prescribed treatment. If the poison cannot be identified, force your bird to swallow egg whites, milk of magnesia, and/or milk.

Petroleum Products, Acids, and Alkalies

Dishwasher detergent	Oven cleaner
Drain cleaner	Paint remover
Floor polish	Paint thinner
Furniture polish	Shoe polish
Gasoline	Toilet bowl cleaner
Kerosene	Wax (floor or furniture)
Lye	Wood preservative

Signs of poisoning caused by these products are bloody regurgitation, loose droppings, shock, depression, coma, convulsions (sometimes), coughing, and redness around the mouth. *Note:* Do *not* induce regurgitation! Make your bird swallow milk, egg whites, or olive oil to prevent absorption of the poison into its system. Then treat for shock.

Acids and alkalies can burn the mouth and skin, so flush these areas with large amounts of water. Apply a sodium bicarbonate paste to acid burns. Apply vinegar to neutralize alkali burns.

Other Known Poisons

Acetone	Carbon tetrachloride
Alcohol	Chlordane
Algae toxins	Cosmetics
Amphetamines	Crayons
Aspirin	DDT
Antifreeze	Deodorants
Arsenic	Detergents
Bleach	

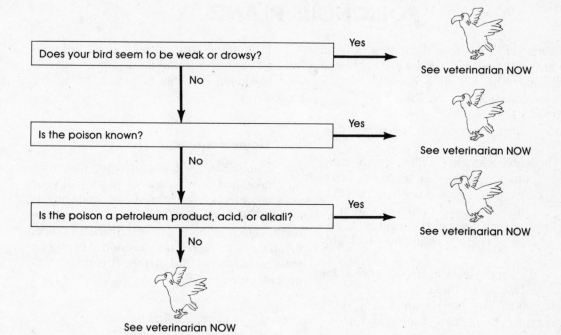

Does your bird seem to be weak or drowsy? — Yes → See veterinarian NOW

No ↓

Is the poison known? — Yes → See veterinarian NOW

No ↓

Is the poison a petroleum product, acid, or alkali? — Yes → See veterinarian NOW

No ↓

See veterinarian NOW

Other Known Poisons (continued)

Fabric softeners
Firecrackers
Fluoroacetates
Garbage toxins
Hair dye
Hexachlorophene (in certain soaps)
Indelible markers
Insecticides
Linoleum (lead salts)
Matches (*Note:* safety matches are nontoxic)
Medicines
Mothballs

Mushrooms (wild)
Paint, lead-based
Perfume
Pine oil
Rat or mouse poison
Red squill
Roach poison
Shellac
Sleeping pills
Snail bait
Strychnine
Suntan lotions
Thallium
Warfarin
Weed killer

Signs of poisoning caused by these products include severe regurgitation, loose droppings, collapse, coma, and convulsions. If your bird is conscious, induce regurgitation: Prepare a mixture of equal amounts of hydrogen peroxide (3 percent strength) and water, and administer a small amount into the back of the throat. A mustard-and-water solution also works well. Repeat until regurgitation occurs, then treat for shock. Inducing regurgitation may cause aspiration, so tilt the bird's head down if it starts to regurgitate.

What to Expect at the Veterinarian's Office

If your bird is unconscious, oxygen and fluids may be given. Other emergency procedures, such as flushing out the crop, may be necessary. Hospitalization will be required.

If your bird is conscious, treatment will depend upon the particular poison swallowed and whether an antidote is known.

POISONOUS PLANTS

Birds that are given flight time around the house may become curious and nibble on houseplants. The following common houseplants are dangerous to your bird:

Christmas cherry: The berry is dangerous.

Dieffenbachia, also called dumb cane: Eating the leaves can cause severe regurgitation, loose droppings, swelling of the tongue, and even suffocation.

Dried arrangements: The seed pods and beans of tropical plants may be highly toxic.

Ivy: Eating the leaves can cause breathing and stomach illness.

Mistletoe: The berries are highly toxic; eating them can cause severe regurgitation, loose droppings, and convulsions.

The following outdoor plants can also be hazardous if chewed and/or swallowed.

Castor bean	Lobelia
Daphne	Mistletoe
Foxglove	Monkshood
Horse chestnut	Nightshade
Jimson weed	Poison hemlock
Larkspur	Water hemlock
Laurels	Yew
Lily of the valley	

In addition, wild birds may eat seeds, worms, and fruit that have been contaminated by pesticides. Weed killers can poison seeds and contaminate the earthworms that birds eat.

Fruit trees sprayed with pesticides can kill fruit-eating birds. Robins and mockingbirds can be killed by the bagworm spray for mulberries.

Home Treatment

EMERGENCY—If you discover that your bird has dined on a poisonous plant, call your poison control center immediately and get veterinary aid. If you don't know the name of the plant, take it along to the veterinarian's office. If you cannot reach a poison control center or your veterinarian, follow the treatment described on page 126.

What to Expect at the Veterinarian's Office

If your bird is unconscious, oxygen and fluids will be given and your bird will be kept warm. The crop may be aspirated to remove any residue of toxin. Hospitalization will probably be required since other life-support procedures may be necessary.

If your bird is conscious, regurgitation will be induced. Treatment will depend on the particular poison and whether the attempts to make your bird regurgitate have been successful.

Prevention

There is one step that you can take to prevent poisoning from houseplants: Do not keep poisonous plants in the house or in the aviary!

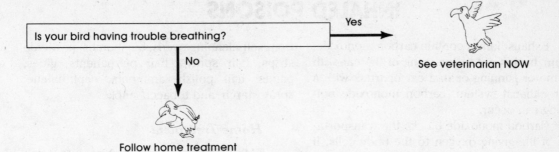

Is your bird having trouble breathing? → Yes

See veterinarian NOW

No

Follow home treatment

INHALED POISONS

Exhaust fumes contain carbon monoxide. If your bird is put in the trunk of the car with the motor running or in a car or truck with a poor exhaust system, carbon monoxide poisoning can occur.

Carbon monoxide blocks the transportation of life-giving oxygen to the body cells. If oxygen cannot get to the cells, death will occur.

The fumes from nonstick cookware or drip pans coated with polytetra fluoroethylene (known as Teflon or Silverstone) are extremely toxic to birds when the pans are overheated (see page 117).

The inhalation of ammonia, naphthalene, or fluoropolymer from spray starch can also kill a bird.

Prevention

Birds are extremely sensitive to inhaled substances. They have a very efficient respiratory system. Watch out for noxious inhalants from self-cleaning ovens, bug bombs, pesticide strips, hair sprays, hair permanents, glues, paints, nail polish, ammonia, naphthalene, spray starch, and tobacco smoke.

Home Treatment

EMERGENCY—Get your bird into fresh air. Seek veterinary assistance at once.

What to Expect at the Veterinarian's Office

If you provided immediate aid, no further treatment may be necessary, and you can probably take your bird home. If not, oxygen (to counteract the carbon monoxide), warmth, fluids, and corticosteroids (to treat any shock) may be needed, especially if your bird hasn't recovered by the time you reach your veterinarian's office. Observation for a few days in the hospital may be suggested if your bird is recovering slowly.

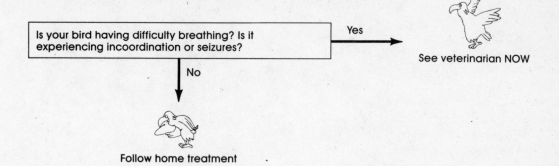

Is your bird having difficulty breathing? Is it experiencing incoordination or seizures?

Yes → See veterinarian NOW

No ↓

Follow home treatment

CHAPTER

8

Common Problems and Diseases

INCREASED WATER INTAKE

Water is essential for all life. Your bird obtains it from eating fruits and vegetables or from drinking. All birds need water. Canaries will die within one or two days without water. Thanks to their centuries of adaptation on the Australian dry lands, budgerigars would be able to go for a longer time without water—but don't test them. Clean, fresh water is needed *every* day for *all* birds. Budgerigars drink about one half to one teaspoon of water daily.

Hot weather, stress, increased exercise, or loose droppings will increase your bird's need for water. Some birds, such as budgerigars and pigeons, will consume more water when they are feeding "crop milk" to their young. In addition, certain medications, such as antibiotics, may cause your bird to become very thirsty. Cockatoos with tapeworms may drink a lot of water.

However, excessive thirst may be a sign of such serious illnesses as diabetes, liver disease, kidney disease, egg-related peritonitis, or uterine infection. Therefore, veterinary attention may be necessary.

Home Treatment

An increased water intake in an alert, active bird with no signs of illness is of no concern. Keep your bird's water cup filled. Clean, fresh water should be provided daily. If there are any signs of illness or if you are concerned about the amount of water consumed, see your veterinarian.

Birds "perspire" by panting, thus losing heat and also water. The water must be replaced by increased water intake. So, if your bird is kept in a very hot room or in direct sunshine, this could cause panting, excessive water loss, and increased water intake.

A new "stress"—a new location, a new family member, or any other environmental change—may make your bird drink more water than normal. So will more exercise—more flight time, for example. Salty foods or medications can also increase your bird's water intake.

What to Expect at the Veterinarian's Office

A complete history and physical examination will be done. If your bird is drinking an increased amount of water, your doctor will test the droppings for sugar (diabetes) by using the *clinitest*. The diabetes that occurs in birds is *treatable*. Most owners of diabetic pets do a remarkable job in giving daily insulin injections. Although diabetic birds cannot be cured (as of this writing, at least), they can still live a normal life. If your bird is diagnosed as a diabetic, please treat it.

Blood tests may be done to further examine the sugar level and to evaluate the liver and urinary system. Cultures will be done to check for infection.

X-rays may be helpful to study the digestive and reproductive systems and kidney size.

Biopsies may also be indicated.

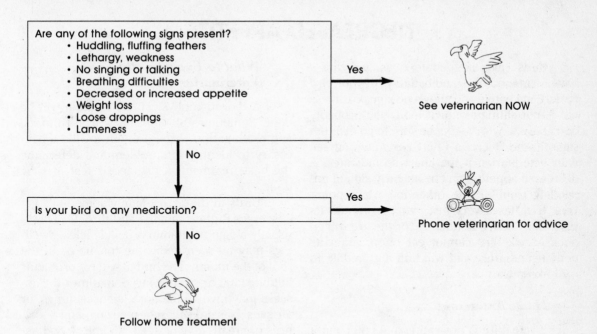

Are any of the following signs present?
- Huddling, fluffing feathers
- Lethargy, weakness
- No singing or talking
- Breathing difficulties
- Decreased or increased appetite
- Weight loss
- Loose droppings
- Lameness

Yes → See veterinarian NOW

No ↓

Is your bird on any medication?

Yes → Phone veterinarian for advice

No ↓

Follow home treatment

DECREASED APPETITE

Birds—just like people, dogs, and cats—have their good days and bad days. If your bird is alert and active and shows no signs of illness but is not eating as much food, you probably don't have to worry—*but* be sure to go over the signs in the Decision Chart *carefully* and see your veterinarian if the chart so indicates. A decreased appetite may be an early sign of impending trouble. One other important point: Your bird has a very *fast* metabolism and its "fire" must be fed frequently (or the fire will go out). A sick bird cannot eat or maintain its body temperature and will fluff and huddle to try to keep warm.

Home Treatment

If your bird is not eating and you cannot see your veterinarian, force feeding may be necessary to provide the calories, nutrients, and water necessary for survival. Also, keep your bird warm. *Note:* Force feeding should *not* be used instead of a veterinary visit. It should be used only in coordination with professional care.

Sometimes environmental changes may change your bird's appetite—new noises, new family members, a new food, change of feed-cup position, a warmer environment. Play detective to find out what may be the problem.

What to Expect at the Veterinarian's Office

A thorough physical examination will be done. Sometimes blood tests, X-rays, cultures, and examination of the droppings will be necessary to identify the problem and determine the best treatment. A psittacosis test may be done.

Birds in the parrot family sometimes get abscesses in their mouths and throats. This is usually a sign of vitamin A deficiencies. Swellings may be seen under the tongue or in the roof of the mouth. The bird may have problems holding food or swallowing. Sometimes the abscess may involve the nose, sinuses, lungs, or air sacs. Nasal discharge, sneezing, and shortness of breath may be seen. Vitamin A and antibiotics may clear up the infection, although a *culture* and *sensitivity* may be needed. Surgical drainage of the abscess is necessary in some cases. If there is only one swelling and no involvement of the respiratory system, your bird has a better chance for recovery.

Cockatiels may exhibit a weakness of the beak and wings that responds to injections of vitamin E and selenium. It is thought to be caused by giardia (see page 182) and an inability to absorb needed vitamins and minerals.

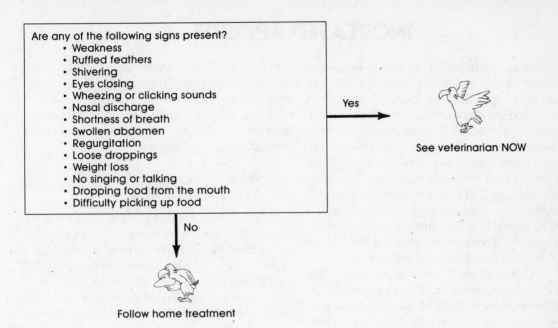

Are any of the following signs present?
- Weakness
- Ruffled feathers
- Shivering
- Eyes closing
- Wheezing or clicking sounds
- Nasal discharge
- Shortness of breath
- Swollen abdomen
- Regurgitation
- Loose droppings
- Weight loss
- No singing or talking
- Dropping food from the mouth
- Difficulty picking up food

Yes → See veterinarian NOW

No ↓

Follow home treatment

INCREASED APPETITE

Increased exercising, a drop in temperature, egg laying, or feeding nestlings will increase your bird's need for food, especially for calories and good-quality protein. However, an increased appetite could mean something else. For example, the early signs of diabetes are increased water consumption, watery droppings, and weight loss despite a voracious appetite. Severe lethargy and weakness are late signs.

Worms and giardia may also cause an increased appetite, although they could equally decrease the appetite or cause no change at all. Still, you should not rule out worms.

A change of food may also increase your bird's food consumption. For example, birds *love* millet sprays and, of course, they will make "pigs" of themselves for these tasty goodies.

If your bird has a voracious appetite and its droppings are watery and dramatic weight loss has occurred, pancreatic, liver, or intestinal trouble may be the cause. These require veterinary attention.

Home Treatment

If you suspect that exercise, environment, or breeding may have increased your bird's caloric and protein requirements, probably no professional treatment will be necessary. You should however, read the section on nutrition (pages 44–45). Any other dramatic appetite changes require veterinary consultation.

What to Expect at the Veterinarian's Office

Your doctor will take the time to get a good history and to perform a complete physical exam. Blood tests, a fecal exam, and a "urine" exam may be needed. Prepare for the visit by *not* feeding your bird in the morning (if it is a morning exam) and by leaving the droppings in the cage so that the doctor can test for diabetes, worms, and giardia.

Remember that most owners of diabetic pets do extremely well in giving the daily insulin injections and checking the droppings. Although the disease cannot be cured (as of this writing, at least), a controlled diabetic can still have a happy life. If your bird is diagnosed as a diabetic, please treat it.

If pancreatic *insufficiency* is suspected, the administration of a pancreatic enzyme may be curative.

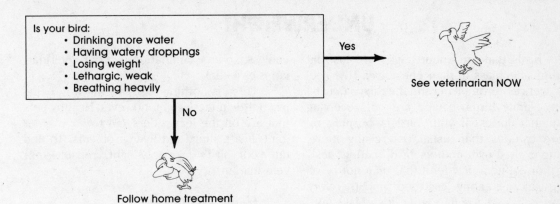

Is your bird:
- Drinking more water
- Having watery droppings
- Losing weight
- Lethargic, weak
- Breathing heavily

Yes → See veterinarian NOW

No → Follow home treatment

UNDERWEIGHT

Birds that are underweight will lose fat and muscle mass in their chest area (the keel will feel very prominent) and the thighs may be thin. Skinny birds usually are not receiving enough calories. If your bird is burning up more calories than usual (exercising more, being excited over another bird, mating, nesting), or eating a new food that may not be as digestible, or eating less food (and therefore fewer calories), weight can be lost. Make sure empty husks have not dropped back into the seed cup—and that the seed cup is really filled with whole seeds. If you have changed the location of the cage, moved recently, brought another pet or appliance (noise) into the house, or had a baby, your bird may be upset and may not eat well. In other words, *any change* (even painting or redecorating) can distress your bird.

But weight loss can occur from medical problems as well. In certain diseases of the pancreas, liver, and intestines, the food is not absorbed properly. (Loose droppings may be present also.) A weight loss accompanied by increased water intake and watery droppings may indicate diabetes, liver, or kidney disease. Intestinal worms are not very common in cage birds but should be checked out. Giardia is common in some birds (see page 68). The list of medical problems that cause weight loss is endless, so an examination by your veterinarian is essential.

There is nothing really wrong with being just a little underweight, however. Healthy pets that are on the lean side seem to have fewer joint, heart, lung, and liver problems. To find out your bird's proper weight, consult your veterinarian.

Home Treatment

If your bird is alert, active, and does not seem ill, you could try increasing the amount of food or changing the food.

Correct any environmental factors revealed in the Decision Chart.

What to Expect at the Veterinarian's Office

If the weight loss is accompanied by signs of illness, or if no weight gain is seen with the increased food intake, see your veterinarian. A complete history and physical examination will be done, and your bird's dietary and excretion patterns will be scrutinized (number, type, and consistency of droppings). Blood tests, a psittacosis test, analysis of a dropping sample, a giardia test, cultures, X-rays, endoscopy, and biopsies may be necessary to find the underlying cause for the weight loss.

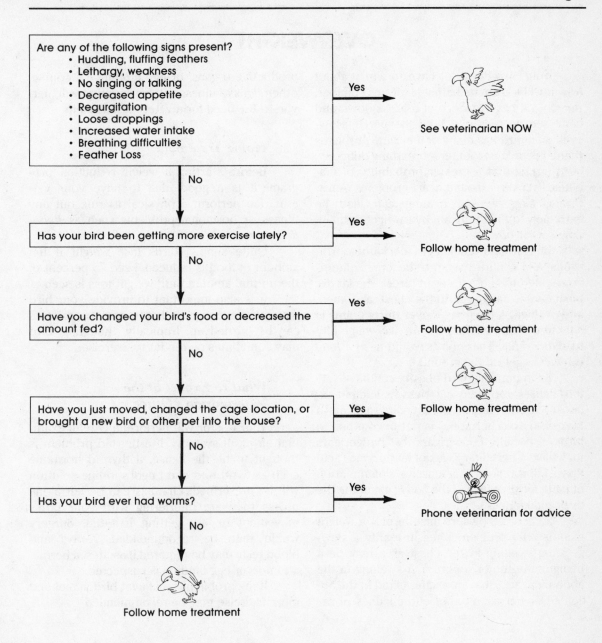

Are any of the following signs present?
- Huddling, fluffing feathers
- Lethargy, weakness
- No singing or talking
- Decreased appetite
- Regurgitation
- Loose droppings
- Increased water intake
- Breathing difficulties
- Feather Loss

Yes → **See veterinarian NOW**

No ↓

Has your bird been getting more exercise lately?

Yes → **Follow home treatment**

No ↓

Have you changed your bird's food or decreased the amount fed?

Yes → **Follow home treatment**

No ↓

Have you just moved, changed the cage location, or brought a new bird or other pet into the house?

Yes → **Follow home treatment**

No ↓

Has your bird ever had worms?

Yes → **Phone veterinarian for advice**

No ↓

Follow home treatment

OVERWEIGHT

Your bird does not have to worry about how it will look in its bathing suit this summer, nor does it have to worry if it looks down and can't see its toes clutching the perch. However, a fat bird has many of the same problems that fat people encounter—breathing difficulty, joint stress, and a greater probability of diabetes, liver disease, and heart problems. Anesthesia, surgery, and healing can also be extremely difficult in an overweight human, dog, cat, or *bird.*

Budgerigars, cockatiels, cockatoos, Amazons, and canaries seem to become "plump" more often than other caged birds. The fat deposits are usually seen in the chest, abdomen, and/or thigh. A budgerigar over thirty grams is a fat bird. Some fat budgerigars may weigh fifty to sixty grams. These birds would need a *long* runway to get off the ground.

As in humans, bird obesity can have various causes: too many calories, insufficient exercise, or heredity. Also, *hypothyroidism* (a lack of thyroid hormone) is not uncommon in birds, especially budgerigars. Fat budgerigars may have a hereditary lack of an enzyme (acid lipase) that results in a massive accumulation of fat in most tissues of the body (including the liver and kidneys).

Sometimes owners misinterpret a weight gain as a fat problem when in reality a slow-growing swelling in the chest area may be a benign fatty tumor (lipoma). A swelling in the abdominal area may be ascites (fluid in the abdomen), a hernia, a tumor of the kidney or reproductive organs, or egg binding. Of course, other signs of illness will be seen that will alert you to the need for a veterinarian's help.

Home Treatment

Before starting a weight-reduction program, it is a good idea to have your veterinarian perform a physical to rule out any illness or hormonal problems such as *hypothyroidism.*

Quite simply, birds lose weight if the amount of food is reduced. Feed 75 percent of the normal amount until weight loss is seen.

It is also important to provide your bird with more exercise so that those extra calories can be burned up. Ironically, though, a bird may sometimes be too fat to exercise.

What to Expect at the Veterinarian's Office

Your doctor will perform a careful examination of all systems. If a thyroid problem is thought to be the cause, a thyroid hormone such as Synthroid and Lugol's iodine solution will be prescribed. Lipomas can be left alone unless they are interfering with your bird's movement or are getting irritated. Surgery would then be recommended. X-rays and blood tests may be required if ascites, a hernia, a tumor, or egg binding is suspected.

If the problem is just a fat bird, a diet and more exercise may be recommended.

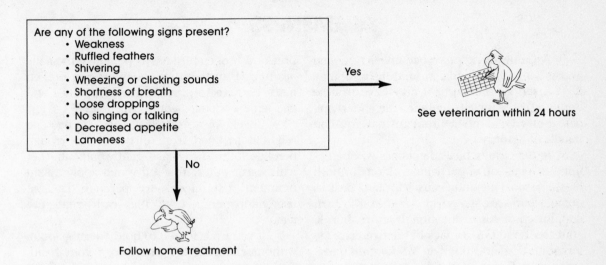

Are any of the following signs present?
- Weakness
- Ruffled feathers
- Shivering
- Wheezing or clicking sounds
- Shortness of breath
- Loose droppings
- No singing or talking
- Decreased appetite
- Lameness

Yes → See veterinarian within 24 hours

No → Follow home treatment

LAMENESS

A "lame duck" may become a "cooked goose." In other words, a limping bird may have a serious illness, or it may have trouble perching and eating. Oftentimes the underlying cause may be a minor problem that you can handle at home.

In the case of birds, lameness will be defined as a lack of, or partial use of, one or both legs. The most common causes for lameness in our pet birds are many: *sore feet* from a torn nail, infection, toe dislocation, fracture, burns, gout (see page 176), or lack of toe exercise; *leg fracture* or dislocation; an *abdominal mass* (usually a tumor of the kidney, testicle, or ovary) pressing on the nerve and blood supply to the legs; a *nutritional deficiency* caused by an improper and unbalanced diet; *arthritis* (or "older-itis," as I heard an old fellow call it) usually seen in older birds or birds standing on improper perches; *head or spinal injuries* that may disrupt "nerve messages" to one or both legs.

Home Treatment

If you have ever had a broken or ingrown nail, you *know* that it is *extremely* painful! Perches that are too small can cause your bird's nails to grow too long, which means that the nails break easily and get caught on things (or worse yet, get caught and cause the leg to break). A broken bird nail is painful. If the nails are long, trim them all, including any broken nails. Be sure to provide proper perches and enough exercise for your bird.

Check your bird's feet. They can become red and irritated from dirty, wet, or rough perches. If this is the case, gently bathe the feet with warm water. Towel dry and apply a skin ointment. Use clean, dry perches. Do not use sandpaper perches; they can irritate the feet.

If you were forced to hold onto this book without changing the position of your hand, your hands and arms would start to hurt and even cramp. Birds that are given perches that are too small or all the same size can get crampy, sore feet. Furthermore, cages that are too small are cruel and are not good for your bird's physical or mental health.

It is very important that all birds—but especially young, growing birds, psittacines, and egg-laying birds—get proper amounts and types of protein, calcium, phosphorus, and vitamins (especially D_3) for proper bone development and health. Any bird that has thick joints, decreased appetite, loose droppings, or problems standing or moving could have a nutritional deficiency (which causes the bones to fracture easily). Prompt and vigorous treatment by your veterinarian is essential. Better

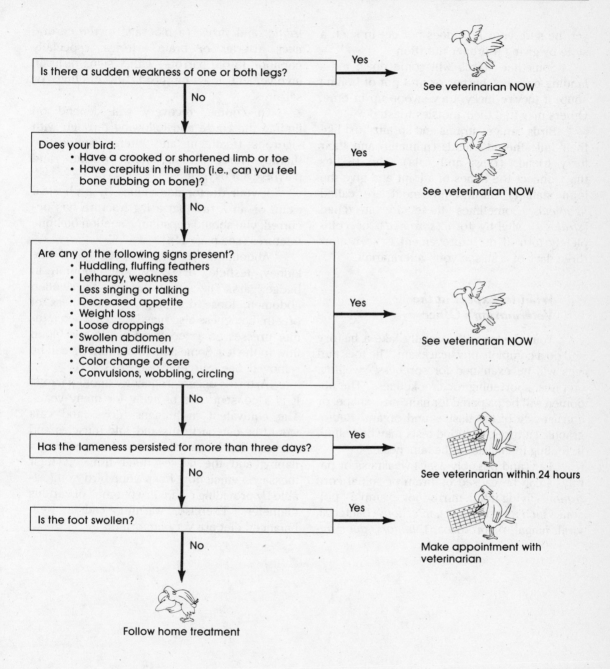

Is there a sudden weakness of one or both legs?

Yes → See veterinarian NOW

No ↓

Does your bird:
• Have a crooked or shortened limb or toe
• Have crepitus in the limb (i.e., can you feel bone rubbing on bone)?

Yes → See veterinarian NOW

No ↓

Are any of the following signs present?
• Huddling, fluffing feathers
• Lethargy, weakness
• Less singing or talking
• Decreased appetite
• Weight loss
• Loose droppings
• Swollen abdomen
• Breathing difficulty
• Color change of cere
• Convulsions, wobbling, circling

Yes → See veterinarian NOW

No ↓

Has the lameness persisted for more than three days?

Yes → See veterinarian within 24 hours

No ↓

Is the foot swollen?

Yes → Make appointment with veterinarian

No ↓

Follow home treatment

yet, be sure your bird does not get in such a state by giving it proper nutrition.

Sometimes birds will come down for a landing on a hot burner or in a pot of boiling soup. If they're lucky, they swoop up in time. Others may find their tootsies toasted.

Birds can get strains and sprains just like their unfeathered friends (humans) and their furry friends (dogs and cats). The tissues that connect the bones of a joint and give the joint stability during movement are called *ligaments.* Sometimes these are stretched (*strained*), slightly torn (*sprained*), or completely torn. If no improvement is seen after three days of rest, see your veterinarian.

What to Expect at the Veterinarian's Office

Your doctor will carefully take a history and do a complete physical exam. The toes and legs will be examined for soreness, swelling, crepitus, shortening, or crookedness. The abdomen will be palpated for pain, size, shape, or consistency of the tissues and organs. Radiographs, cultures, or blood tests may be helpful in finding the cause of the lameness.

Leg (and possibly wing) weakness or paralysis can be caused by brain or spinal cord *trauma* (flying into a mirror, for example), poisons (such as lead paint), *infections* (bacterial, viral, fungal, or protozoan), *tumors, poor nu-trition,* and *stroke* (a blockage of the carotid neck arteries or brain arteries, especially common in old parrots). Other signs of brain involvement may be head tilt, circling, or seizures.

Of course, recovery will depend on finding the cause and following through with vigorous treatment and intense supportive therapy—force feeding, fluids, warmth, and maybe even oxygen.

If your doctor determines by a physical exam or an X-ray that a leg fracture has occurred, you should consult the section on bone fractures (see page 118).

Abdominal tumors, especially of the kidney, testicle, or ovary, are common in budgerigars. The symptoms may be swollen abdomen, loose droppings, or shortness of breath. Lameness also may be seen when a tumor presses on a nerve and blocks the blood flow to the leg. Some abdominal tumors can be removed. See "Surgery" (page 81).

Arthritis occurs frequently in old parrots. It is a consequence of living for many years. The equivalent in humans, dogs, and cats would be osteoarthritis and "old muscles and nerves." The joints get creaky, the muscles get flabby, and the nerves don't transmit their messages efficiently. Keep your bird comfortable by providing clean, dry perches of various diameters. Exercise, warmth, and a well-balanced diet are very important.

ALLERGIES

Birds may have allergies. Straining, flatulence (passing of gas), inflammation of the cloaca, or sneezing may be seen. Of course, it is important to rule out the most common causes of these problems, but think about possible allergies—the blanket that covers the cage? the sunflower diet? a perfume, household spray, or dish detergent used around the birds? a "treat" that you are giving the bird? some food in the diet? cigarette smoke? Go over an environmental and food checklist with your avian veterinarian.

LUMPS AND BUMPS

Birds get lumps and bumps just as we and our dogs and cats do. Most are benign (not malignant or cancerous).

The most common lumps and bumps of our bird friends are brown hypertrophy of the cere; white, crusty material around the eyes and beak, caused by cnemidocoptic mange; lipomas (fatty deposits, especially common to budgerigars, rose-breasted cockatoos, and canaries); crop swellings; gout (white deposits in the joints); hematomas; abscesses; feather cysts; subcutaneous emphysema; and malignant tumors.

Home Treatment

If your bird has free-flight time, it may fly into an object and break some blood vessels under the skin. The swelling that results is called a *hematoma.* Birds don't have a great supply of blood, so it is probably best to let the hematoma be resorbed. No treatment is necessary.

Birds get abscesses. They are usually hot, painful, reddened swellings, but they are not soft like our "boils." An abscess is a walled-off

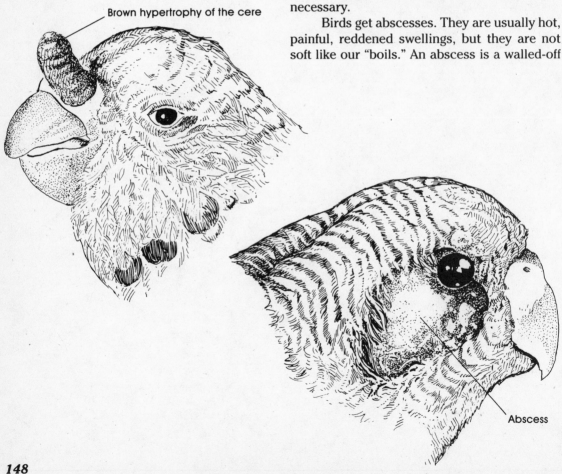

Brown hypertrophy of the cere

Abscess

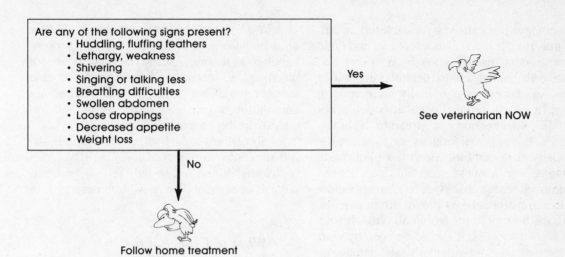

Are any of the following signs present?
- Huddling, fluffing feathers
- Lethargy, weakness
- Shivering
- Singing or talking less
- Breathing difficulties
- Swollen abdomen
- Loose droppings
- Decreased appetite
- Weight loss

Yes → See veterinarian NOW

No → Follow home treatment

collection of pus caused by a bacterial or fungus infection. It is a collection of live and dead bacteria, dead tissue, white blood cells, and other cells called on to defend your bird's body. An abscess is potentially dangerous: If prompt medical and/or surgical attention is not provided, the infection can spread to the lungs, air sacs, brain, heart, kidneys, or liver via the bloodstream. Since birds don't have liquefying enzymes, the abscess material is "cheesy." Common areas for abscesses to form are below the eye in psittacines, in the mouth in parrots, or on the bottom of the feet in all birds. If your bird has an abscess, it should be seen by your doctor, since the potential for tissue damage or death from bacterial toxins is high unless proper wound cleaning and/or surgery and antibiotic treatment are done.

If it is impossible for you to see a veterinarian, you will have to treat the abscess at home. If the abscess is open and draining, probe and clean the wound with a cotton-tipped applicator. Remove any matter that may be in the wound and squeeze out the "cheesy" material. Using an eyedropper, squirt a small amount of hydrogen peroxide (3 percent) into the wound, three times daily. Press on the swelling to help the hydrogen peroxide flush the wound.

If the abscess has not burst, apply hot washcloths to the area to help bring it to a head. When you can feel a soft spot in the swelling, nick it with a clean razor blade. Probe and flush the wound as explained above. Try to get your bird on antibiotics as soon as possible.

Note: At times what looks like an abscess on a budgie's foot is actually a gouty tophus. Lancing a tophus usually results in severe bleeding, so consult a veterinarian if you suspect gout. The disease results from an accumulation of uric acid in the joints and frequently in the internal organs.

Sometimes a bird will rupture an air sac if it flies into an object. A swelling that has a "crackling" sound will be felt. Usually no treatment is necessary. The air will be resorbed.

What to Expect at the Veterinarian's Office

If the tumor is a benign one, such as a *lipoma* (fatty tumor) of the chest or thigh, your doctor will probably advise no treatment unless it becomes irritated. Any suspicious skin growth should be removed and biopsied. Sometimes swellings will form above or below the cloaca. X-rays help in diagnosing this problem. If the swelling is above the cloaca, it is usually a hernia. If it is below the cloaca, it could be a tumor, egg binding, or hernia. Egg bindings, some tumors, and some hernias are treatable. Feather cysts are seen most frequently in canaries and macaws. Although they can appear anywhere, the wing is a common site. They can usually be removed surgically.

Abdominal hernias in budgies ordinarily occur in females and are related to degeneration of abdominal muscle related to female hormones. An abdominal hernia is difficult to repair due to degeneration of muscle.

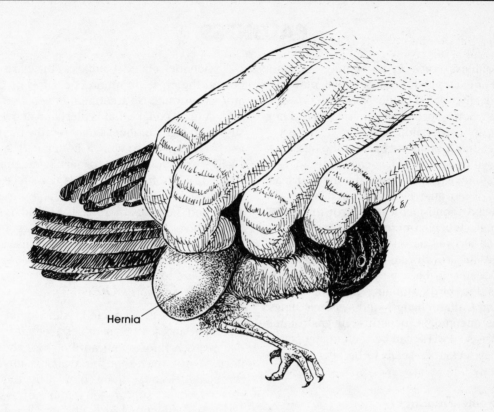

Hernia

BALDNESS

Baldness "runs in the family" of some birds. For example, lutino cockatiels may have a genetically related baldness on the crown of the head. Some species of canaries have a hormone-responsive baldness.

Feather loss on the back of the head may be caused by an aggressive cagemate.

Psittacine beak and feather disease (PBFDS) syndrome is a serious disease that may include abnormal feather growth (curled, deformed, clubbed, or constricted feathers) on the head as well as on the body. "Beak rot" (changes in growth and color) may be seen. PBFDS seems to be a viral disease that suppresses the bird's immune system, causing beak and feather changes and systemic illness such as pneumonia, hepatitis, or gastrointestinal disease. PBFDS can be seen in any parrot, although cockatoos seem to be affected more frequently.

Home Treatment

If an aggressive bird is "playing woodpecker" on a cagemate, separate them. Keep an eye on the "picked on" bird (Look for signs of illness; see page 107). Frequently the bird is sick, and the natural instinct of the flock (especially lovebirds) is to kill the sick one.

Genetic-related baldness (the bare spot behind the crest) in lutino cockatiels or cockatoos is normal. No treatment is necessary.

A male canary that is alert and active and shows no signs of illness may regrow the head feathers, especially with a better diet (pages 44–51) and some real or artificial sunlight (page 42). If home treatment is not successful, testosterone can return a male canary to song and good head feathering. It should not be used if liver disease is suspected; long-term testosterone dosage can *cause* liver disease.

What to Expect at the Veterinarian's Office

If PBFDS is suspected, your doctor may take skin and feather samples to confirm the diagnosis. A fluorescent antibody for the suspected virus may soon be available for early screening. Because many birds with this disease have a suppressed immune system, secondary infections are common. Treatment involves antibiotics, antifungals, autogenous vaccines, gammaglobulin preparations, immunostimulants, and any other supportive care to keep your bird nourished and comfortable.

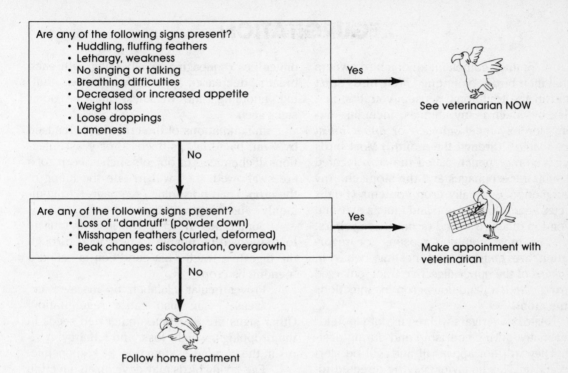

Are any of the following signs present?
- Huddling, fluffing feathers
- Lethargy, weakness
- No singing or talking
- Breathing difficulties
- Decreased or increased appetite
- Weight loss
- Loose droppings
- Lameness

Yes → See veterinarian NOW

No ↓

Are any of the following signs present?
- Loss of "dandruff" (powder down)
- Misshapen feathers (curled, deformed)
- Beak changes: discoloration, overgrowth

Yes → Make appointment with veterinarian

No ↓

Follow home treatment

REGURGITATION

A common complaint among bird owners is that their bird is "vomiting." Well, birds don't vomit in the traditional sense. (Vomiting is a reflex by which many animals, including humans, forcibly repel *stomach or upper intestinal contents* through the mouth.) Most birds have a storage pouch called the *crop* located between the esophagus and the stomach. Any regurgitation is usually crop contents (fluids, mucus, and/or food). Food and mucus may end up on top of a bird's head or on the cage bars.

The most common reasons for regurgitation are courting and nesting behavior, blockage of the upper digestive tract, enlarged thyroid gland, a pendulous crop, or infections of the crop.

Male budgerigars will regurgitate food for their mates during courtship and during nesting. They will not appear ill and will be alert and active. This behavior may be directed toward a toy, a mirror (the bird's own image), or even the bird's owner. For example, a parrot may attempt to "feed" its owner with a dramatic display of head and neck bobbing, and by opening its mouth (but usually without any regurgitation of food).

Birds can gorge themselves with grit, which results in a blockage (impaction) of the crop; they may also swallow anything that catches their curiosity. If such foreign objects obstruct the upper digestive tract, actual (or attempted) regurgitation will result.

Goiter, or enlargement of the thyroid glands, is not uncommon in budgerigars. A diet of seeds deficient in iodine may cause enlargement of the thyroid glands, which press on the esophagus. Regurgitation will result. Breathing difficulties (squeaking or wheezing with each breath), decreased appetite, weight loss, fluffing, huddling, and weakness may be other signs seen.

Inflammations of the crop can be caused by viral, bacterial, psittacosis, or yeast infections. If chemicals or objects such as corn cobs are swallowed, they will irritate the lining of the crop. Lead poisoning (see page 126) commonly causes regurgitation.

Sometimes the crop will lose its muscle tone and will be unable to pass food through the digestive tract. This condition is called a "pendulous crop."

Proventricular dilatation, or "macaw wasting disease," can also cause regurgitation. Other signs are diarrhea, undigested seeds in the droppings, weight loss, and lethargy. A virus in the nervous system may be responsible.

Egg-laying birds may develop an infection in the uterus or an egg peritonitis. Regurgitation may be seen.

Home Treatment

If your bird is "courting" a mirror or some other object, you can stop the "love affair" by removing the object. If the display is directed at you or another family member—well, just feel glad that your bird is so affectionate.

Some birds will gorge themselves with grit—especially if they have a gastrointestinal upset (which is a behavior perhaps similar to dogs with upset stomachs eating grass). Administering a few drops of mineral oil and gently squeezing the crop may help break up the impaction.

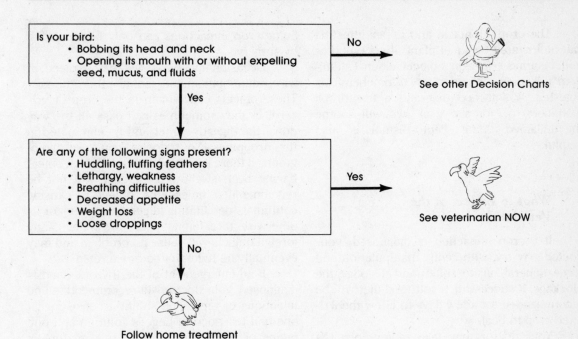

Is your bird:
- Bobbing its head and neck
- Opening its mouth with or without expelling seed, mucus, and fluids

No → See other Decision Charts

Yes ↓

Are any of the following signs present?
- Huddling, fluffing feathers
- Lethargy, weakness
- Breathing difficulties
- Decreased appetite
- Weight loss
- Loose droppings

Yes → See veterinarian NOW

No ↓

Follow home treatment

The crop, stomach, and upper intestine can be irritated by small plant fibers (such as millet sprays), foreign objects eaten (aluminum foil, pieces of bone, etc.), or chemicals ingested. A soft-food diet and a few drops of mineral oil for a day or two will soothe the inflamed lining. Pepto-Bismol is also helpful.

What to Expect at the Veterinarian's Office

If a crop impaction is diagnosed, your doctor may try, with gentle manipulation and some mineral oil, to soften and dislodge the blockage. If successful, a soft-food diet will be recommended for a few days to allow the irritated crop to heal.

Your doctor may take radiographs (X-rays) to see the type and extent of blockage.

Some crop impactions can only be corrected by surgery.

Occasionally, birds will eat a piece of wire, aluminum foil, or some other "no-no." These objects can remain in the crop or gizzard, or they sometimes can pass all the way down the digestive tract and be eliminated in the droppings. Your doctor can take radiographs if there is a suspicion of a foreign object having been swallowed. Surgery will not be recommended unless the object is causing continual, debilitating digestive upsets or is otherwise threatening your bird's life. Many foreign objects will cause no problem and may eventually be regurgitated or excreted.

If an enlargement of the thyroid gland is diagnosed, your doctor will recommend iodine injections or an iodine solution consisting of one-half teaspoon of Lugol's solution and one ounce of water. One drop of this mixture is mixed in one ounce of drinking water (for budgerigars) for two weeks. One drop of this mixture can be placed once weekly in the drinking water to prevent recurrence.

Soft foods and antibiotics will be prescribed if a bacterial infection of the crop is suspected.

Budgerigars can develop a pendulous crop (cause unknown). The crop loses its muscle tone, and a saclike swelling flops over the breast area filled with seed, mucus, and fluid. Your doctor will show you how to hold the bird upside down and gently milk out the crop contents. Soft food and antibiotics may be prescribed.

Radiographs will be taken if proventricular dilatation or lead poisoning is suspected. Blood tests, a psittacosis test, cultures, endoscopy, urinalysis, and fecals may be needed to evaluate the bird's total condition.

Hospitalization with intravenous or sub- cutaneous fluids, a warm hospital cage, and medications may be recommended.

Prevention

To prevent the swallowing of foreign objects, keep an "eagle eye" on your bird when it takes its daily exercise out of the cage. Keep coins, wire, and other "delicacies" away from parrots' perches and be sure that flight cages do not have any loose wire strands.

Introduce small amounts of grit to a bird that has not had any for a while—since grit gorging and impaction may occur.

To prevent enlargement of the thyroid gland, one drop of the Lugol's/water mixture described above can be placed in the drinking water once weekly. A well-balanced, varied diet helps.

Watch out for lead-based objects!

LOOSE DROPPINGS

One of the most common bird problems that I see in my practice is loose droppings. A bird's droppings are a mixture of "urine" and feces. Loose droppings can thus be caused by a problem in the digestive tract, its associated organs (liver, pancreas), or the urinary tract. Bacterial, psittacosis, yeast (candida), and giardia infections are very common. Dietary or environmental changes can also produce loose droppings.

The normal droppings of most birds are targetlike in shape and consist of a black or dark green firm part (feces) and a softer white part ("urine"). A bird should have between twenty-five and fifty eliminations per day. The majority should be the target variety, although a few shapeless, watery droppings should not be of any concern unless other signs of illness are seen. The droppings of fruit eaters and mynahs are normally loose.

Home Treatment

Medications can cause side effects. So if your bird is taking any medicine, call your veterinarian to see if it may be causing the loose droppings.

Sometimes a new brand of bird food or a newly opened package of food, treat, or cuttlebone, or too many greens or fruits, etc., can cause loose droppings. Since our city water supplies are not the healthiest (containing chemicals, etc.), purchase distilled water in your drugstore and see if the droppings become firm. Keep the water refrigerated once it is opened.

Table foods, especially those that are spicy, can irritate the digestive tract. If you stop feeding your bird this type of food and give it some Pepto-Bismol, the loose droppings should stop.

Birds are nibblers—so if they are allowed to fly free in your home, keep a careful eye on them. Some paints and plaster contain lead. Lead poisoning (page 126) can cause loose droppings—or worse—convulsions, blindness, and death. Birds can recover from lead poisoning if treated early by a doctor.

Anything is "fair game" for the free-flying bird—houseplants, soap, Christmas decorations (tinsel, cellophane, string, ornaments). If you suspect that your bird has eaten something harmful or has other signs of illness, call your veterinarian for advice.

A pet owner consulted with me about a cockatoo that had loose droppings for a month. I made a house call and we played detectives. Working with the Decision Chart, we discovered that an aerosol (furniture polish) was used almost daily on a china closet *next to the bird*. Stopping the spray stopped the loose droppings. Stop all aerosols for a week or two to see if the droppings improve. Many chemicals are not good for us *or* our birds.

Stress, Stress, Stress. Yes, stress can cause diarrhea in birds. Of course, their nerves don't get rattled from traffic jams, the world news, or an impending final exam, but a new cage location, drafts, new family members, and new noises are big events to a bird. More—or less—exercise or attention and stressful or long training sessions can cause nervous diarrhea. You will notice that loose droppings will occur when your bird is taken for a ride to the

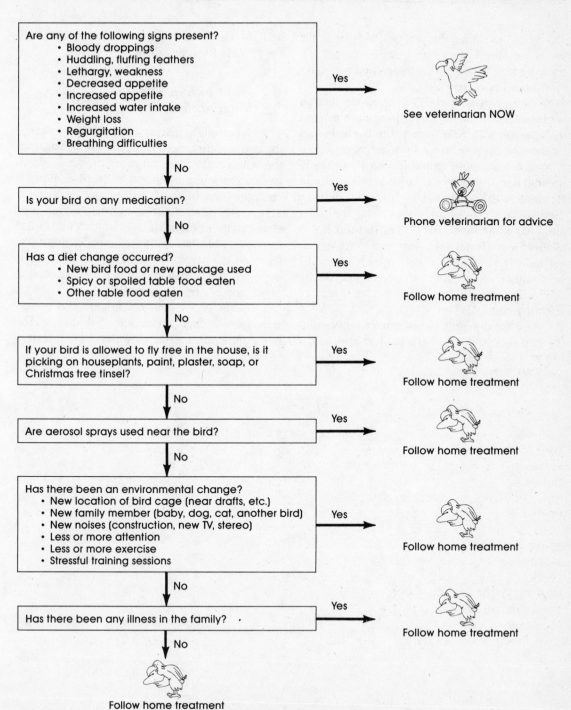

Are any of the following signs present?
- Bloody droppings
- Huddling, fluffing feathers
- Lethargy, weakness
- Decreased appetite
- Increased appetite
- Increased water intake
- Weight loss
- Regurgitation
- Breathing difficulties

Yes → See veterinarian NOW

No ↓

Is your bird on any medication?

Yes → Phone veterinarian for advice

No ↓

Has a diet change occurred?
- New bird food or new package used
- Spicy or spoiled table food eaten
- Other table food eaten

Yes → Follow home treatment

No ↓

If your bird is allowed to fly free in the house, is it picking on houseplants, paint, plaster, soap, or Christmas tree tinsel?

Yes → Follow home treatment

No ↓

Are aerosol sprays used near the bird?

Yes → Follow home treatment

No ↓

Has there been an environmental change?
- New location of bird cage (near drafts, etc.)
- New family member (baby, dog, cat, another bird)
- New noises (construction, new TV, stereo)
- Less or more attention
- Less or more exercise
- Stressful training sessions

Yes → Follow home treatment

No ↓

Has there been any illness in the family?

Yes → Follow home treatment

No ↓

Follow home treatment

veterinarian's office. Put yourself in your bird's shoes (or should I say on your bird's perch); try to eliminate possible stresses and see if the droppings improve.

Birds can become ill from some human bacteria. Some of our sore throats are caused by a "staph infection"—and this bacteria can be spread to your bird from a sneeze or a cough. A bacterium called *E. coli* is normally present in our intestines, but it is *not* a normal resident in the intestines of birds. So be sure that you wash your hands after using the toilet and before handling your bird or its food. If you suspect a bacterial infection, see your veterinarian—these bacteria can spread to your bird's other organs, and can even cause death. Antibiotics are necessary for the treatment of such infections.

If your detective work hasn't pinpointed the cause, and if your bird is alert and active and shows no other signs of illness, try some Kaopectate for a few days.

What to Expect at the Veterinarian's Office

A complete history will be taken to see if the cause is dietary or environmental. The doctor will conduct a complete physical exam, paying particular attention to the abdomen for enlargements of the liver, kidney, or sex organs. Sometimes tumors, hernias, or retained eggs can press on the intestinal tract and cause infrequent but large eliminations. Radiographs (X-rays) are helpful in deciding which organ is enlarged. If a bird is urinating a lot, a complete urinalysis is very important.

Birds, especially budgerigars and cockatiels have a high incidence of diabetes. The early signs are increased water intake, watery droppings, weight loss, and a voracious appetite. If your doctor suspects diabetes, the *clinitest* will be used to test the droppings for sugar. A blood sugar test is also helpful for diagnosis. Insulin controls the diabetes in birds—just as it does in humans, dogs, and cats.

A culture and sensitivity of the droppings are recommended since *E. coli* and other enteric organisms, if present, can be the cause of the loose droppings. A psittacosis test may be done. Antibiotics will help clear up this condition.

Of course, a microscopic exam for worm eggs and giardia should be done whenever loose droppings are seen.

Other blood tests, such as phosphorus and uric acid, are helpful if kidney involvement (inflammation, gout, or early tumor) is suspected. Radiographs may also be helpful in pinpointing the cause of the loose droppings.

Fatty infiltration of the liver, possibly an enzyme (acid lipase) deficiency, is fairly common in birds. (An enlarged liver can be felt by examining the abdomen and can be confirmed by X-rays.) The birds lose weight and have loose droppings. Convulsions may also occur. The affected bird should have the other tests discussed above to rule out diabetes, gout, and other problems. Endoscopy and biopsy may also be helpful for diagnosis.

Prevention

Birds are creatures of habit. Be considerate when changing *anything* in the home.

Keep a careful eye out for harmful plants or objects that may be swallowed by your bird when it is out of its cage.

Wash your hands before handling the bird, its food, or its toys.

All new birds should be isolated (quarantined) from your established birds for thirty to sixty days. See "Aviculture Management," pages 200–201.

CONSTIPATION

Constipation is not common in birds. The causes may be grit gorging, eating of foreign objects, pasting of the vent, or pressure on the rectum caused by a tumor, retained egg, or hernia.

Constipation is characterized by straining when droppings are passed or by having infrequent droppings. (Birds should have twenty-five to fifty droppings per day.)

Home Treatment

"Pasting of the vent" (the droppings paste against the vent so further eliminations are impossible) can be caused by poor diet, poor hygiene, or loose droppings. Clean the vent area with soap and warm water. If the vent area is irritated, apply a skin ointment.

A gastrointestinal upset can cause grit gorging (in the same way that dogs with upset stomachs eat grass). Administering a few drops of mineral oil is helpful, as is eliminating all grit for a few days, then slowly increasing the amount back to normal.

What to Expect at the Veterinarian's Office

If your bird has impacted feces trapped in the rectum, your doctor will *palpate* the abdomen. In addition, an X-ray may be suggested to study the extent and cause of the impaction.

Soapy warm-water enemas and mineral oil (administered orally) are helpful for simple constipation. Your veterinarian should discuss diet and hygiene requirements for your bird.

If a mass such as a retained egg, tumor, or hernia is preventing elimination, surgery may be necessary. Retained eggs, if located in the lower oviduct, may be removed by dilating the female canal with forceps and instilling mineral oil.

Prevention

Be sure that your bird gets proper exercise and that the cage and nest are kept clean. Lack of exercise and overeating can cause obesity in your bird—and an obese bird will more readily encounter such problems as poor muscle tone and constipation problems.

As your bird ages, so does the muscle in the intestine, which becomes lazy and moves the feces through the intestines much more slowly. The longer the feces stay in the intestine, the more water is removed from them, making the droppings much drier and less frequent.

Greens and fruits—washed thoroughly and given in moderation—are great natural laxatives. Be sure that your bird's water container is always filled because adequate fluid intake is very important.

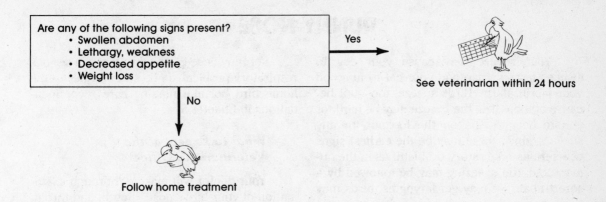

Are any of the following signs present?
• Swollen abdomen
• Lethargy, weakness
• Decreased appetite
• Weight loss

Yes

See veterinarian within 24 hours

No

Follow home treatment

RUNNY NOSE

Your sneeze may cause your dog to awaken from its nap and your cat to jump off your lap in alarm. Birds sneeze, too—but because of their size, the sneeze may be hard for you to hear. So be on the lookout for any sneezes, since these may be the earliest signs of a serious respiratory problem. As in the human cold, the sneezing may be followed by a sore throat (we may get laryngitis, birds may have change of voice or song) and coughing (in birds, a "click" is heard). You may see the feathers stained brown around the nostrils if your bird has a runny nose.

Runny nose in birds is commonly caused by an infection (virus, bacteria, psittacosis, or fungus). Sometimes a seed, gravel, or some regurgitated material lodged in the nostril can cause sneezing or a discharge. Aerosol sprays used near a bird can also cause irritation, such as sneezing or nasal discharge, of the respiratory system. Nasal tumors are not common in birds.

If your bird has a discharge from the eyes and/or nostrils and is huddling and fluffing feathers, appearing lethargic, shivering, and breathing heavily, a serious respiratory infection may be present.

Home Treatment

Restrain your bird. Shine a light into the nostrils to see if a seed or some dirt, gravel, or regurgitated material has settled there. Use a small thumb forceps, a few hard bristles from a brush, or one "tooth" of a fine-tooth comb to remove any such obstruction.

If aerosols may be causing the problem, you should, of course, stop using them or avoid using them near the bird's cage.

A runny nose can be the start of a serious respiratory problem, so be sure to refer to the home bird hospital nursing care recommendations in Chapter 5.

What to Expect at the Veterinarian's Office

Your doctor will make a thorough examination of your bird's nose, mouth, and throat. A speculum is handy for examining the bird's upper airway.

Most respiratory infections in birds (as in humans, dogs, cats, etc.) are viral, with bacteria finding a "home" to do more damage. Early infections are best treated with antibiotics administered by mouth and/or by injection. If your bird is alert and active and is eating, your doctor may let you treat your pet at home with antibiotics, vitamins, warmth, and rest (twelve hours of darkness).

Ideally, whenever a respiratory infection is seen, a bacterial and fungus culture (see "Laboratory Tests" in Chapter 4) and an antibiotic sensitivity should be done on the nasal or throat discharge for bacteria or fungi so that the proper medicine can be used. X-rays may also be taken. A psittacosis test may be done.

If the infection involves the sinuses, there will be swelling and loss of feathers around the eye and a nasal discharge. Flushing of the sinus with sterile water and antibiotics is necessary.

Birds that have serious respiratory infections benefit from hospitalization—oxygen and heat can be provided in an incubator and proper nutrition by tube feeding. Some doctors feel that nebulization (a mist of water and/or medicine droplets) is also beneficial. Birds do get sick just like we do—and do need good

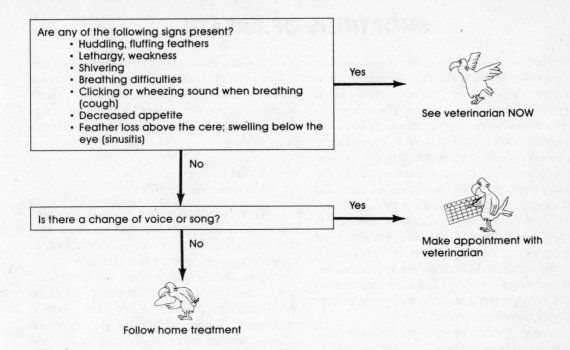

Are any of the following signs present?
- Huddling, fluffing feathers
- Lethargy, weakness
- Shivering
- Breathing difficulties
- Clicking or wheezing sound when breathing (cough)
- Decreased appetite
- Feather loss above the cere; swelling below the eye (sinusitis)

Yes → See veterinarian NOW

No ↓

Is there a change of voice or song?

Yes → Make appointment with veterinarian

No ↓

Follow home treatment

nursing care to get them through the crisis of an illness.

Prevention

Isolate new birds for one month before placing them near your bird.

Be sure that your bird is eating a balanced, nutritious diet (see "Nutrition," Chapter 3).

Be sure that all cages and food and water containers are kept clean and disinfected.

Keep your bird away from drafts and drastic fluctuations in room temperature.

Look for *early signs* of respiratory infection—a sneeze, a slight nasal discharge, or a staining of the feathers around the nostrils.

Do not place the bird's cage near an air conditioner or heater.

Avoid using aerosols near the bird's cage.

SHORTNESS OF BREATH

Birds will breathe rapidly in hot weather or in a warm room to regulate their body temperature. They also will breathe rapidly when they are frightened or nervous. These are normal body reactions—*not* shortness of breath. If your bird is truly having trouble breathing in or breathing out and is gasping for breath, there is probably a serious obstruction in the chest, breathing tubes, lungs, or air sacs. An abdominal enlargement from a tumor, peritonitis, or fluid (ascites) can also cause shortness of breath by inhibiting full expansion of the breathing system. The normal breathing rate for small birds such as finches, canaries, and budgerigars is 80 to 125 breaths per minute; for larger birds such as parrots it is normally 40 breaths per minute.

Some birds (especially canaries and finches) can have tracheal and air sac mites. You will hear a clicking respiration. Shortness of breath usually indicates that there is infection or a generalized infection. Abdominal enlargements from tumors and peritonitis (from a ruptured egg) or thyroid gland enlargements (in budgerigars) are also common. Birds also can get heart problems.

Home Treatment

The breathing rate of a bird that is frightened, nervous, or fatigued from exercise should return to normal a few minutes after such activity stops.

New noises, new animals in the home, or a new location can disturb a bird's respiratory patterns.

If a caged bird is kept in direct sunlight, it can get overheated—causing it to breathe rapidly—and can collapse from heatstroke. Moving the bird to a cooler location and out of direct sunlight will return the panting bird to a normal state.

What to Expect at the Veterinarian's Office

Your veterinarian will perform a careful physical examination of all systems. Your bird may need warmth and oxygen. Veterinarians may use an incubator for this purpose.

Your doctor will consider the most common causes of shortness of breath: bacterial infections, viral or viruslike infections (such as psittacosis), fungus infections (such as aspergillosis), air sac mites, abdominal tumors and swellings, or thyroid gland enlargement.

Laboratory tests, electrocardiograms, and X-rays are helpful in making a diagnosis. Your veterinarian will probably want first to stabilize your bird's condition with warmth, oxygen and fluids.

All birds with labored breathing benefit from oxygen and warmth. Bacterial infections are treated with antibiotics. Nebulization (vaporizing) may be helpful. Psittacosis, air sac mites, and aspergillosis are treated with special drugs. Many sick birds do not eat well, or they will stop eating entirely. A bird's metabolism is very fast—like a furnace. If the coal (food) is not provided, the fire goes out. Your doctor will consider tube feeding your bird. This is a safe and gentle procedure in which a

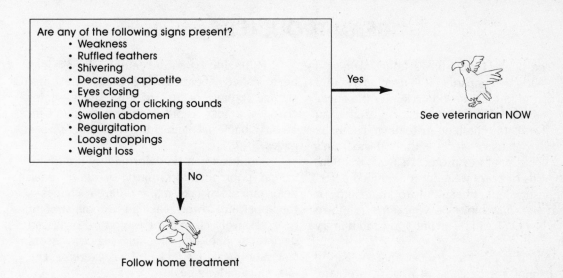

Are any of the following signs present?
- Weakness
- Ruffled feathers
- Shivering
- Decreased appetite
- Eyes closing
- Wheezing or clicking sounds
- Swollen abdomen
- Regurgitation
- Loose droppings
- Weight loss

Yes → See veterinarian NOW

No

Follow home treatment

flexible tube is placed into your bird's mouth and upper digestive tract and a nutritious mixture is emptied into the crop. This mixture contains most of the water, protein, fats, carbohydrates, calories, vitamins, and minerals that your bird will need to maintain its life and to heal properly.

If the shortness of breath is caused by a thyroid gland enlargement (common in budgerigars), injections of sodium iodine and an iodine solution in the water can cure the "goiter" (see "Home Pharmacy," page 90). Some abdominal tumors can be removed surgically with good results. Birds with shortness of breath caused by allergies respond very well to steroids.

BEAK TROUBLES

The beak is your bird's knife, fork, and spoon—and its chopstick! It is used as a scoop for water, a nut and seed cracker, and a slicer for greens and vegetables. It is also used as an extra "hand" for climbing or feeling. The beak is a fine defensive (to bite the veterinarian's finger occasionally or protect its nest) or offensive (birds of prey) weapon. It is indeed a versatile instrument of beautiful workmanship (or is that work*bird*ship?). So you can see, a bird with a bad beak will be an unhappy and hungry bird.

All birds have a very fast metabolism. If they cannot eat because of a beak problem, they will lose weight rapidly—10 to 20 percent of their body weight daily! They will not be able to maintain their high body temperature—thus, they will ruffle their feathers, huddle, and become inactive. If the beak problem is not corrected, they may die.

Psittacine beak and feather disease has been called "beak rot" because the first changes may occur in the beak—color changes, cracks, rapid beak growth, and secondary bacterial and fungus invaders (see pages 70–73).

The beak can be deformed by a mite invasion, poor nutrition, injury, or tumor. Beak deformities can take many different shapes—the upper and lower beak can become straight or excessively curved, or the entire beak can deviate to one side—looking like a scissors ("scissors-beak"). A lack of "beak exercise" can also cause a long beak.

The microscopic cnemidocoptes mite can invade and destroy some of the beak's growth tissue. Whitish crusts will be seen on the beak, the corners of the mouth, the eyelids, and even

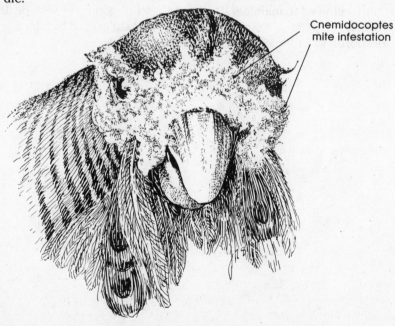

Cnemidocoptes mite infestation

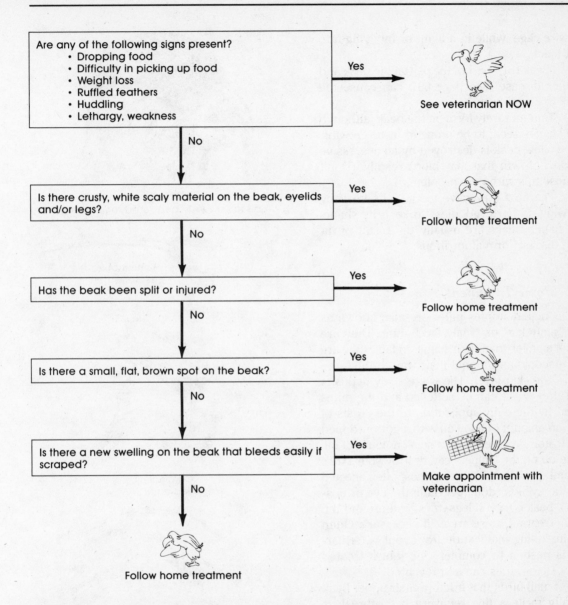

Are any of the following signs present?
- Dropping food
- Difficulty in picking up food
- Weight loss
- Ruffled feathers
- Huddling
- Lethargy, weakness

Yes → See veterinarian NOW

No

Is there crusty, white scaly material on the beak, eyelids and/or legs?

Yes → Follow home treatment

No

Has the beak been split or injured?

Yes → Follow home treatment

No

Is there a small, flat, brown spot on the beak?

Yes → Follow home treatment

No

Is there a new swelling on the beak that bleeds easily if scraped?

Yes → Make appointment with veterinarian

No

Follow home treatment

on the legs and cloaca. If not treated in time, the mite will destroy some of the beak's growth tissue and will cause the beak to become deformed.

A bird's beak is remarkably adapted for obtaining the smorgasbord of food that the bird needs to survive in the wild. *You* are depended upon to provide that well-balanced, nutritious diet in the home environment. Insufficient protein or excess vitamin A can contribute to beak deformities.

Occasionally, a bird will injure its beak on

its wire cage, while in a fight, or by flying into an object.

"Beak rot," part of the psittacine beak and feather disease (see page 69), can cause the beak to crumble away.

Tumors rarely form on the beak, although budgerigars seem to be prone to these growths. The yellow beak is destroyed by an aggressive reddish growth that may bleed readily. (Don't confuse this with cere problems.)

The bird may have to "jog" its beak by chewing on hard "goodies" to keep its shape. Misshapen beaks are usually the result of injury, disease, or malnutrition.

Home Treatment

Cnemidocoptes mites are also known as the "scaly leg" or "scaly face" mite. They are much smaller than their name. In fact, they are microscopic and tunnel their way through the bird's top skin layer. The white scaly deposits that they make can be softened and the mites killed by the daily application to the crusts of a *small* amount of baby oil with a cotton-tipped applicator. Be sure to use a small amount of oil, since oil on the feathers can destroy your bird's natural insulation. The areas most often affected are the eyelids (don't get oil in the eye or nostrils), beak corners, legs, toes, and around the vent. Treat all these areas, if necessary. Often a mite-killing medication from your veterinarian is needed to complete the job. If treated early, deformities can be prevented.

Small birds that fracture their upper beak usually make a fine recovery if the break is treated early. Wrapping a few layers of adhesive tape around the beak for three weeks should keep the beak stable so that it will heal nicely. Small breaks may need no stabilization if the bird can eat. The small break will grow out like a fingernail.

Parrot
eats large seeds; beak used for climbing

Hummingbird
nectar eater

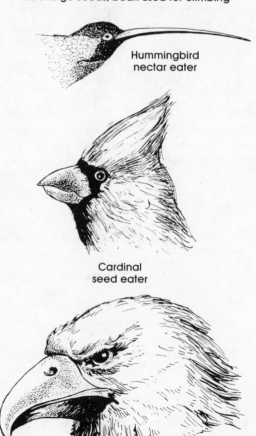

Cardinal
seed eater

Eagle
meat eater; beak used for tearing flesh

Beak fractures in larger birds may require extra support. Plastic (from a plastic cup) or a pliable metal cut to the beak's size and shape can be used as a splint and taped to the beak for three weeks.

Occasionally a flat, brown spot will appear on the beak and remain there without getting larger. Don't worry! It is thought to be caused by a temporary inflammation (from injury or illness) to the beak's growth cells and blood vessels—similar to the black spot that appears on your nail if a hammer hits it.

Be sure to provide a cuttlebone or lava stone for your bird to help keep its beak trim.

What to Expect at the Veterinarian's Office

Your veterinarian will conduct a complete physical exam. If your bird is weak, lethargic, and puffed-up, and has lost considerable weight, the doctor may recommend hospitalization for warmth (in an incubator) and tube feeding (to build up its strength). This may also be done at home.

If the beak is deformed, your doctor will suggest a treatment regimen based on the cause of the beak trouble. If the cnemidocoptes mite is the problem, medication will be given. If the beak is already deformed from the mite infestation, it should be trimmed frequently so your bird can eat properly. An infected bird should be isolated from other birds. It is a good idea to wash down the cage with warm water and soap. If treated early, your bird will make a fine recovery. The mite spends its complete life cycle on birds and does not like humans or other animals. Cnemidocoptes is not usually transmitted between cages, so birds caged separately should be safe. See page 152 for a discussion of psittacine beak and feather disease.

If poor nutrition is the cause of the beak deformity, your doctor will discuss the proper diet and supplements for your bird.

Some beak fractures require extensive wiring. Sometimes an upper or lower beak is beyond repair because of illness or injury. Your doctor may recommend frequent trimming so your bird can eat properly. Moistened instant baby cereals, greens, vegetables, dry dog food or bird pellets (crushed), and vitamin or mineral supplements can be used if your bird has problems grasping seeds. If needed, a prosthetic or "artificial" beak can be made for your bird. If psittacine beak and feather disease is suspected, special tests will be done (see page 70).

Beak tumors are uncommon, and when they do occur, they are usually malignant. Your doctor can biopsy the mass to determine if the growth is benign and if surgical removal will be necessary.

Prevention

Keep your bird's beak healthy by providing proper nutrition, beak exercise (cuttlebone or lava stone), trimming if necessary, and sanitation (regular cage cleaning).

Isolate new birds for one month before placing them with your other birds.

Isolate and treat any bird showing signs of cnemidocoptes (scaly face, scaly leg) mite. Clean the cage.

Be sure to cover mirrors and windows when your bird flies around your home. The beak is the first thing to hit in a midair collision.

Any animals that are not socialized to your bird should be kept away during its free-flying time. Unusual loud noises such as the afternoon soap operas and the vacuum cleaner should be prohibited during flight time. Otherwise, your bird may be frightened in flight and may bruise itself.

CERE PROBLEMS

Many birds have a prominent, fleshy structure called a cere at the base of the upper beak. The cere houses the nostrils and probably has a role in the sense of touch. In mature male budgerigars, the cere is blue in color; in females, it is pink or brown. Sexually immature budgerigars have a pinkish-brown cere.

A whitish crust sometimes forms on or around the cere. If you do not treat this early, the beak will become deformed. Cnemidocoptes mites are the culprits with this problem.

Sometimes the cere of psittacines (especially female budgerigars) will become very thick, hard, and brown. Called brown hypertrophy (*hyper* = great; *trophy* = growth), the condition is not "cere-ious" unless it blocks the nostrils.

The cere may become involved in a sinus infection. A cheesy or liquid nasal discharge will be seen, and the cere will appear quite swollen.

A tumor of the testicle will occasionally cause the cere of the male budgerigar to change from blue to brown. This will be accompanied by other signs such as weakness, decreased appetite, labored breathing, swollen abdomen, loose droppings, or paralysis of one leg if the tumor is pressing on a nerve.

Home Treatment

Cnemidocoptes mites can be treated effectively (the mites killed and no beak distortion) if caught early.

You can soften the growth of brown hypertrophy by applying *boric acid ointment* for three days and then gently scraping the softer growth with your fingernail or filing it gently. Or, you can do nothing. It will grow back. Repeat the procedure. If the overgrowth starts to block the nostrils, see your veterinarian.

What to Expect at the Veterinarian's Office

Since a change in the size or color of the cere can be an outward warning of a serious internal problem, your veterinarian will do a complete physical examination, lab tests, and X-rays. Fluids, warmth, and oxygen will be given if needed.

Sinus infections sometimes respond to antibiotics alone, although surgical drainage is usually needed.

Most testicular tumors are usually not evident until they grow very large and cause symptoms such as breathing difficulties. Birds with these tumors are usually poor surgical risks, and the location of the tumor makes safe removal difficult but not impossible. Surgical removal can be attempted if the tumor is detected early.

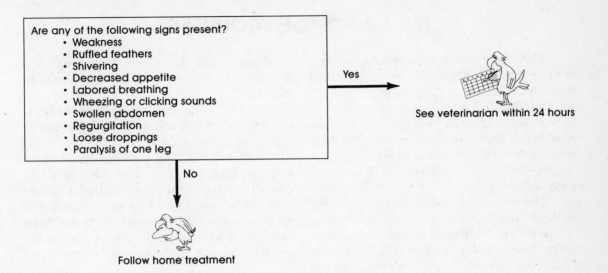

Are any of the following signs present?
- Weakness
- Ruffled feathers
- Shivering
- Decreased appetite
- Labored breathing
- Wheezing or clicking sounds
- Swollen abdomen
- Regurgitation
- Loose droppings
- Paralysis of one leg

Yes

See veterinarian within 24 hours

No

Follow home treatment

NAIL AND TOE TROUBLES

Birds have a multitude of uses for their nails—scratching, fighting, holding and tearing food (or the veterinarian), perching, climbing, and even cleaning their feathers.

A bird's nails, just like ours, continuously grow from a basal germ layer and can be damaged or deformed by disease, injury, or lack of preventive care (exercise, cleanliness, and good nutrition).

Cnemidocoptes mites can invade and damage your bird's nail beds, causing deformed claws. The characteristic whitish crusts around the beak, corners of the mouth, eyelids, legs, or cloaca will be a tip-off that the mite wants to make its home in your bird.

Anyone with long nails knows the painful feeling of bending or breaking one. Birds are vulnerable to the same pain.

Bacterial infections of the nail bed (from injury, dirty cages, or dirty perches) can cause swelling of the nail bed and damage to the growth area. Ultimately, the nail will grow out deformed. Bacterial infections and Vitamin A deficiencies can cause "bumblefoot"—infection of the foot.

Home Treatment

If a nail is bleeding from injury, gently apply direct pressure for a few minutes on the nail with a gauze pad to stop the bleeding. Styptic powder or household flour can also be used. *Remember:* Loss of a *few* drops of blood lost by us is not a problem, but it can be *catastrophic* to a small bird since its blood volume is so small—gentle handling is thus important to avoid shock. Be sure to keep your bird in a quiet, dark, and warm spot, and observe it frequently for weakness, shortness of breath,

huddling, or ruffling feathers. By the way, if a nail does not regrow, it will be no handicap to your bird.

Crusty, white scaly material on the beak, eyelids, and/or legs will tip you off that cnemidocoptes mites are present.

Crooked nails are the final result of injury, nail-base infection, mite infestation, incorrect perch size, or poor nutrition. Crooked nails can take the form of spirals or corkscrews or even more exotic shapes. Frequent trimming and adequate perch size for normal toe and nail exercise are necessary. Large perches

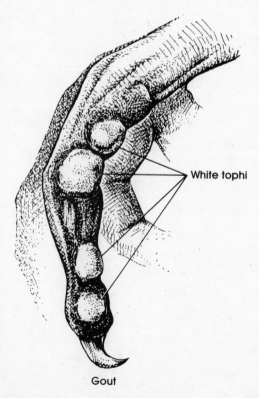

White tophi

Gout

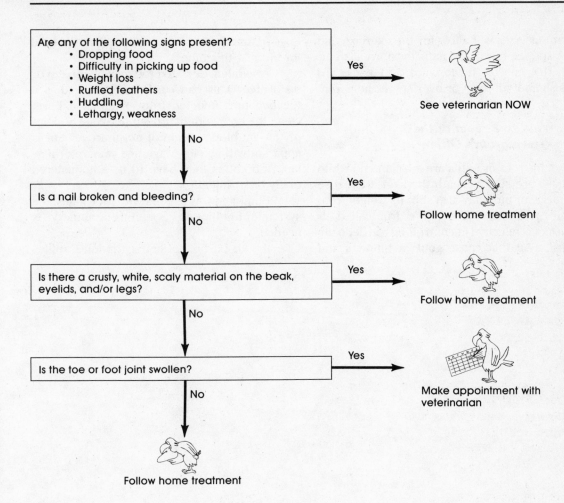

Are any of the following signs present?
- Dropping food
- Difficulty in picking up food
- Weight loss
- Ruffled feathers
- Huddling
- Lethargy, weakness

Yes → **See veterinarian NOW**

No

Is a nail broken and bleeding?

Yes → **Follow home treatment**

No

Is there a crusty, white, scaly material on the beak, eyelids, and/or legs?

Yes → **Follow home treatment**

No

Is the toe or foot joint swollen?

Yes → **Make appointment with veterinarian**

No

Follow home treatment

in various sizes will allow for toe exercise and more surface to rub the nails for normal wear.

The tips of the forward and backward nails should not meet or overlap on the perch.

What to Expect at the Veterinarian's Office

If the toes or joints are swollen and white deposits are seen beneath the skin, the cause is gout. Your bird may also shift its weight from one leg to another. Although a drug called allopurinol is effective in controlling the deposits of uric acid that cause gout in humans and dogs (dalmatians), the treatment is not helpful for birds at this time.

A swollen, deviated toe may be broken or dislocated. This can easily be stabilized. If a toe becomes infected from a cut or a burn, clean the area with hydrogen peroxide and apply an antibiotic cream. If no improvement is apparent within a few days, see your veterinarian. Antibiotics may have to be administered orally or by injection.

Bumblefoot is treated with foot soaks and systemic antibiotics. Sometimes surgery is needed.

If your bird is not eating, huddles, ruffles

its feathers, and is lethargic and weak, it may have serious *systemic* problems and may need your veterinarian's help.

Prevention

Be sure that there are no unsafe projections of wire, etc., that may catch your bird's legs in its cage or aviary.

Provide perches of various sizes for good toe exercise and nail wear. To determine an adequate size, check that the tips of the forward and backward nails do not meet when your bird perches.

Disinfect the perches weekly. Examine the *bottom* of your bird's feet frequently.

During flight time, be sure that your bird is kept away from the stove (boiling liquids and hot burners).

Normal nail (keratin) growth depends on proper nutrition—especially the right type and amount of amino acids and vitamin A.

Clean perches of various sizes (to exercise the toes and help keep the nails trim) are very important. Fruit trees (those not sprayed with chemicals) such as apple or pear are fine perches. Oval perches are better than round perches.

EYE SWELLING OR DISCHARGE

Your bird's eyes can be affected by bacterial, viral, or mite infections or by a deficiency of vitamin A. They can also be injured or irritated. Frequent blinking, closing of the eye, redness, discharge, or swelling of the eyelids will alert you that the eyes are involved.

Viral, fungal, psittacosis, and bacterial respiratory infections are very common in birds. Eye discharges, runny noses, "clicks," or "wheezes" may be early signs. Be sure to watch for these oftentimes subtle signs.

Our old friend the cnemidocoptes mite must be included here also since the whitish crusts produced can irritate the eyelids and eye.

Aerosol sprays, projections such as wire, or bird fights can injure or irritate the eyelid or eye. Occasionally, foreign material (dusty seed, for example) in your bird's eye will cause an irritation.

A sinus infection, vitamin A deficiency, or an abscess can cause swelling around the eye. Tumors behind or within the eye are rare in birds, although benign cysts of the eyelid are occasionally seen and can be removed surgically.

Home Treatment

If your bird has an eye discharge from a mild irritation but is alert and active and eating well, the short-term use of 5 percent boric acid ophthalmic ointment, Neosporin, or Neopolycin is recommended. Clean the debris gently with warm water and a cotton ball and then apply the ointment. Keep your bird warm and free of stress, and be sure it eats and has at least twenty-five well-formed droppings daily.

If an aerosol spray irritated your bird's eyes, discontinue using the spray. Birds are very sensitive to our twentieth-century technological "advances."

Be sure that your bird gets enough vitamin A.

What to Expect at the Veterinarian's Office

Your veterinarian will check vision, as well as the eyelids, the inner eye, and the reaction of the pupil to light with a special magnifier called an *opthalmoscope,* which has its own light source. A green dye called fluorescein is used to determine if the cornea is healthy. A complete physical, blood tests (including a psittacosis test), cultures, and radiographs may also be done, since an eye problem may be part of a systemic disease.

Antibiotic eyedrops or ointments are given for eye infections. Injections of antibiotics, vitamin A, and oral antibiotics are also frequently helpful.

Humans get "chicken pox" and birds get "bird pox" (not contagious to humans). Canaries and Amazons seem to be highly susceptible. A whole flock of canaries can be wiped out from "canary pox" in a few weeks. A thickening of the eyelids (and sometimes the legs) caused by reaction to the pox virus is the outstanding sign. The thickened sores will also spread to the mouth and respiratory system. There is no specific treatment. Sick birds, which can recover, should be isolated and the bird premises cleaned.

Psittacine pox is currently a great problem and the cause of many eye infections.

Sometimes a sharp projection or a fight with another bird can tear the eyelid. Direct pressure will stop the bleeding.

If sutures are not necessary, an ophthal-

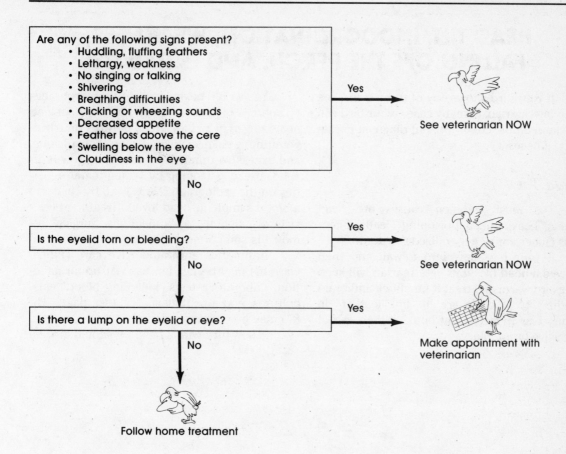

Are any of the following signs present?
- Huddling, fluffing feathers
- Lethargy, weakness
- No singing or talking
- Shivering
- Breathing difficulties
- Clicking or wheezing sounds
- Decreased appetite
- Feather loss above the cere
- Swelling below the eye
- Cloudiness in the eye

Yes → See veterinarian NOW

No ↓

Is the eyelid torn or bleeding?

Yes → See veterinarian NOW

No ↓

Is there a lump on the eyelid or eye?

Yes → Make appointment with veterinarian

No ↓

Follow home treatment

---

mic eyedrop may be prescribed to avoid infection. Occasionally, sutures are necessary to allow proper healing.

Eye surgery is performed if the eye has been severely injured and must be removed. Removal of an eye (which is called *enucleation*) should not bother your caged bird, and it should stay happy as a lark (or a parrot, or whatever). Cataracts are not uncommon in older birds. A white object will be seen where the pupil should be. A caged bird does not need its sight and should be able to function with cataracts. Of course, if you are near a veterinary school that has a veterinary ophthalmologist who is experienced in the removal of bird cataracts (it's much easier in the larger parrots), by all means make arrangements for a consultation.

Sinus infections may also take frequent flushing or surgery to clear up.

HEAD TILT, INCOORDINATION, WEAKNESS, FALLING OFF THE PERCH, AND PARALYSIS

If your bird shows any of these signs, see your veterinarian. In many cases, your bird will have a *treatable* condition, but diagnostic tests may be necessary.

Head Tilt

The most common causes are head trauma, heavy metal poisoning (lead), infections (inner ear or generalized), or tumors.

If your bird flew into a wall and then showed a head tilt, your veterinarian will keep your bird warm and treat it for shock and brain swelling. Most birds are in "fine feather" in twenty-four to forty-eight hours if there is not extensive brain injury.

You would be amazed at the environmental sources of lead (see page 126). Signs of lead poisoning may include green or black diarrhea, vomiting, weakness, wing droop, convulsions, and excessive thirst. Your veterinarian will diagnose lead poisoning by seeing metal densities on the radiograph (X-ray) and by checking a blood sample for lead levels. Treatment consists of calcium EDTA injections. Surgical removal is sometimes necessary.

Antibiotics and supportive care (fluids, warmth) may be needed to clear up an infection. Laboratory tests, including blood tests, cultures, and a psittacosis test (see pages 81–87) may be recommended.

A new bird with a head tilt should also be

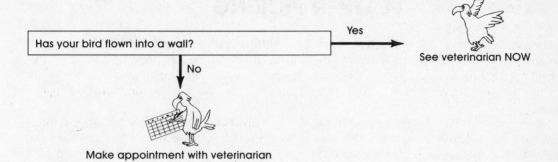

| Has your bird flown into a wall? | → Yes → See veterinarian NOW |

No ↓

Make appointment with veterinarian

checked for Newcastle disease, a disease that could wipe out the chicken or turkey industry.

Incoordination

Infections, toxicities (such as lead), tumors, and vitamin deficiencies can produce a wobbly bird.

Weakness/Falling off the Perch

A weak grip can be a sign of a generalized infection, poor nutrition, a vitamin E/selenium deficiency (especially in cockatiels), fractures, nerve damage, arthritis (especially in older parrots), gout (with parakeets), low blood calcium (African greys), loose perches, tight leg bands, or tumors (especially in parakeets).

Paralysis of One Leg or Both Legs

The most common causes are abdominal tumors (with parakeets; see "Surgery," page 81), infections, trauma (fractures, sprains), and vitamin E/selenium deficiency (with cockatiels). Egg-laying females may be egg bound, have a fracture from a calcium deficiency, or have a nerve weakness from a difficult delivery.

FEATHER PICKING

If your bird is normal and healthy, it will preen and groom by cleaning its feathers, applying oil from the preen gland (if present), and removing the protective sheaths from new feathers.

When your bird has feathering problems, you and/or your avian veterinarian must play detective to find the cause. For example, a juvenile hand-raised bird that has an unkempt appearance may have never been taught to preen.

Abnormal feather growth may, in many instances, be caused by a disease. Among the most common causes are psittacine beak and feather disease (PBFD), "French molt" (budgerigar PBFD), or other viral diseases that alter feather growth. Herpes virus or adenovirus infection of lovebirds is not uncommon.

Feather picking can have many causes: sexual picking; internal disease; malnutrition; boredom or nervousness; giardia; bacteria, yeast, or fungus infection in the feather follicles; skin parasites; hormonal imbalances; viruses; or overzealous mate preening.

You and your veterinarian must work together. Keeping a good history, knowing the species of the bird (each species has its most common feather problems), and getting a medical workup are helpful (see pages 81–87).

When birds make their nests, they prepare the brood patch by removing the feathers from their chest, abdomen, and legs. This featherless area will keep the eggs warm. This behavior is seasonal and depends on increased hormone levels. Your bird does not have to be around eggs to do this sexual picking. It is most common in grey cheeks, conures, African greys, and cockatoos. Hormones and a collar are the treatments of choice.

Birds eating a poor diet (seed diet) suffer from malnutrition. Improving the diet improves the skin and feathering in three to six months (see the section on nutrition, pages 44–51).

Parrots are very playful, social, and intelligent creatures. If they don't receive attention, loving care, toys, and exercise, they will pick their feathers (like nail-biting humans).

Emotional and psychological picking may require the services of a *qualified* avian behaviorist. Ask your avian veterinarian for recommendations.

To alleviate bird boredom, spend more *quality* time with your bird. Also, leave a radio, TV, or tape on when you are not at home. Toys such as *American* (white) rawhide, chains, swings, ladders, bells, mirrors, and branches are appreciated. Move the cage to different areas of the house during the day, and include your bird in family activities. Provide a larger cage or place on a perch *out* of the cage. Adequate rest, ultraviolet light (Vita-lite or Duro-lite), and bathing (see page 51) keep the feathers in good shape. Chewy foods such as carrots and broccoli provide nutrition and "busy work." Your veterinarian may collar your bird initially to break the picking cycle. "Psychological" picking, it must be emphasized, is only thought to be important after your doctor has ruled out the other causes or if only the unreachable head feathers look perfect. It is most commonly seen in grey cheeks, conures, African greys, and macaws.

Giardia, an intestinal parasite, seems to be an important factor in cockatiel and, less so, budgerigar feather picking. Your veterinarian will perform a trichrome giardia test and, if positive, treat your bird.

Skin or feather follicle infections (bacteria, fungus, or yeast) respond nicely to many of the newer-generation antibiotics, yeast, or fungal medications. Your doctor can make the diagnosis by a gram stain or culture and sensitivity of the feather pulp from a new (blood) feather.

Skin parasites are not common in pet birds except for the cnemidocoptes mite of budgerigars and the itchy mite of grey-cheek parakeets. Both are treatable by your veterinarian. Do not use the mite sprays or mite discs available commercially. Lice infestations are rare in pet birds.

An enthusiastic cagemate may pick a bird's feathers (especially on the head). Separate them for a while.

Some viruses are often incriminated: psittacine beak and feather disease; feet gnawing from herpes virus in macaws and cockatoos; and wing web or feet mutilation in (pox) lovebirds, Amazons, small macaws, and African greys. Antiviral drugs may be helpful, as well as new generation antibiotics.

Hormonal imbalances or feather cysts are occasionally associated with feather picking.

As you can see, the diagnosis and treatment of feather picking can be difficult. Have patience and work with your veterinarian. A medical workup must be done to rule out the many causes of feather picking. Improvement can be seen in a few weeks or several months.

A few foul-tasting sprays that sometimes help decrease feather picking are Bitter Apple spray, or dilute Listerine sprayed on the feathers (avoid the eyes). These are not cures. Find out the *underlying* problem.

SCREAMING

Roosters crow when the sun rises or sets. Parrots have a modified crow—but not *cocka-doodle-doo*. Many parrots scream to greet the day and to wish everyone a good night.

The parrot yell or scream can also be a greeting or an expression of discontent. A parrot that screams *all day* or *all night* is a stressed bird. Stress can contribute to illness.

Home Treatment

If your bird only screams at sunrise and sunset, remove the food six to eight hours before the onset of screaming and offer it just before the loud vocalizations begin. It is important that the bird *not* be fed in response to the screaming. If the bird is not hungry, you can try offering a toy, giving more exercise, or moving the bird closer to you before the screaming starts.

If your bird screams when you return home, go directly to the bird and provide attention and perhaps a favorite toy that was withheld during the day.

Moving the bird to a new location or isolating it from the family's activities may cause screaming. Try to perch the bird so that it feels included in the family life. Introducing your bird gradually to a new location with patience, play, and kindness will be appreciated.

What to Expect at the Veterinarian's Office

Your veterinarian will help you identify the source of your bird's problem. If there are concurrent signs of illness, blood tests, cultures, and radiographs (X-rays) may be performed.

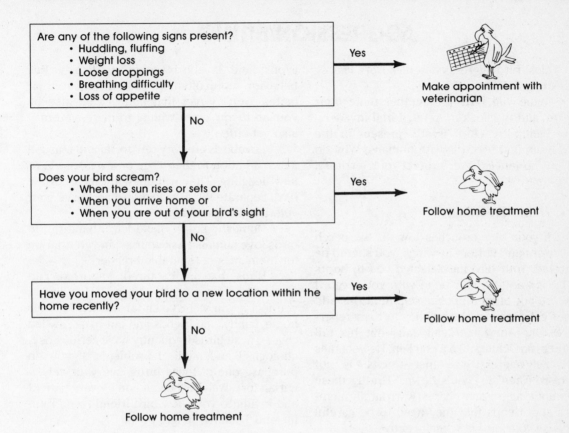

Are any of the following signs present?
- Huddling, fluffing
- Weight loss
- Loose droppings
- Breathing difficulty
- Loss of appetite

Yes → Make appointment with veterinarian

No ↓

Does your bird scream?
- When the sun rises or sets or
- When you arrive home or
- When you are out of your bird's sight

Yes → Follow home treatment

No ↓

Have you moved your bird to a new location within the home recently?

Yes → Follow home treatment

No ↓

Follow home treatment

AGGRESSION/BITING

Most bird aggression comes from fear or is sexually related.

In the wild, birds protect their mate, their babies, and the flock from territorial invaders. This "computer chip" is still present in the bird brain just like it is with humans. Why do we put up fences? We "protect" our territory, of course.

Home Treatment

If your bird crouches low on the perch and raises and flutters its wings, you should be flattered. Your bird has selected you to be its mate. It wants to pair bond with you, even if you are not of the opposite sex. Amazons add other cute "pickup" techniques to their repertoire. Our Amazon, Cacul, fans out his tail feathers and clucks like a chicken. He becomes extremely aggressive to others when he is "hot to trot." Then he "cools down." During these prenuptial aggressive phases, warn family members and friends that they need to be careful because your bird is sexually active.

If your bird is showing extreme aggression to other birds in the cage or to its mate, separate them. Captive male cockatoos have been known to kill their mate because she is not receptive or because their own sexual energy lacks the natural outlets of nest selection and defense. Confine the female in a neighboring cage until she is receptive. Cockatoos, Am-

azons, and lovebirds seem to display this behavior more often to other birds or their mates. Don't forget that mate could also be you; so if you're not willing to mate, you may also get bitten.

Lovebirds are very territorial and may kill a new addition to their cage or a weak, sick, or new fledgling. They will chew the head of the bird. Separate the attacked bird and have your veterinarian examine it.

Domestic-bred, hand-fed, hand-raised birds love humans. Ask your avian veterinarian for the names of reputable breeders.

Birds that are captured, imported, and quarantined are severely stressed. How would you feel if you were taken far away from your home, family, and friends and put in a crowded cage? These birds frequently have serious psychological and medical problems. If you do purchase one of these birds, see your veterinarian for a well-bird exam and be very patient and loving to your new bird friend (see "Taming and Training," pages 57–60).

What to Expect at the Veterinarian's Office

A thorough physical examination will be performed to see if there is a medical reason for your bird's aggression. If so, the appropriate laboratory tests, including a blood lead level and X-rays, may be ordered.

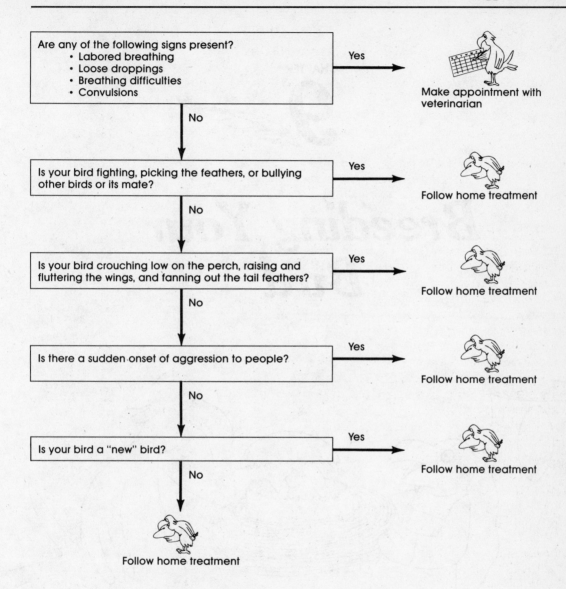

Are any of the following signs present?
- Labored breathing
- Loose droppings
- Breathing difficulties
- Convulsions

Yes → Make appointment with veterinarian

No ↓

Is your bird fighting, picking the feathers, or bullying other birds or its mate?

Yes → Follow home treatment

No ↓

Is your bird crouching low on the perch, raising and fluttering the wings, and fanning out the tail feathers?

Yes → Follow home treatment

No ↓

Is there a sudden onset of aggression to people?

Yes → Follow home treatment

No ↓

Is your bird a "new" bird?

Yes → Follow home treatment

No ↓

Follow home treatment

Breeding Your Bird

"IT'S A GIRL"

Delivery Tree

PLAYING MATCHMAKER

Birds may not need candlelight and a nice wine to fall in love, but they do need a compatible mate, the proper nest, good nutrition, and a little help from you.

Canaries

The Breeding Cage

A double or triple breeder cage is used to introduce the cock and hen formally. The breeding cage has a divider made of wood or wire mesh. The cock and hen are kept separated for a few weeks until they feel familiar with the breeding cage and with each other. You can purchase a wire, plastic, or ceramic nest in pet shops, or you can make a wooden nest box or use a soup strainer with its handle removed. Hang the nest box halfway down the side of the cage so that the nestlings can lift their heads and their parents can perch on the side of the nest and feed them comfortably.

The First Date

In northern climates, the "dating season" begins around March 1—springtime—when everyone's fancy turns to you-know-what.

How do you know that the "date" is going to work out? When the male begins to call the female and to feed her through the bars, you've become a certified matchmaker! Remove the partition. Without referring to *The Joy of Sex,* the male will soon start mounting or "riding" the female, and nature will take care of the rest.

The Nest

Commercial nesting material or straw, hay, fresh grass (without insecticides on it), cotton, feathers, or dried moss can be used. If the hen starts to pick up feathers or other material in her cage, she needs nesting material. Long pieces of string or thread should not be used since the parents or youngsters can get tangled in it.

Egg Sitting

The mother canary will usually lay one egg daily. Her *clutch* (or total egg group) will be two to six eggs. Since it is much easier for her if all the eggs hatch at the same time, replace each egg with a dummy egg, available at pet shops. Gently place the real eggs on a piece of cotton. (You may find it easier to move them with a tablespoon.) Gently turn the eggs over daily. The dummy eggs can be replaced by the real eggs after the hen lays the last one.

The male can be left with the female if he seems helpful and does not bother

her. Otherwise, remove him and return the wire divider to the cage. If she seems upset in his absence, return the father-to-be.

The New Arrivals

In about *two weeks,* you will be grandparents!

Soft food is needed for mother to feed to her new babies (or nestlings). Nestling food is available commercially. You can also add the yolk of a hard-boiled egg or some bread dipped in boiled milk. The soft food should be kept in a separate cup from mother's regular seed cup. Be sure that the soft-food cup is never empty (the babies are big eaters). Every time they gape, the mother and father must stuff the soft food down their throats. Be sure that the soft food does not go stale.

Weaning

The chicks' eyes will open in one week. Their feathering and perching ability will be well along at three weeks. The babies can be separated from their parents at four weeks of age. Soft food is provided along with their normal seed mixture. If at first they are having trouble cracking seeds, you should crack, but don't crush, the seeds with a rolling pin. Soaking the seeds for twenty-four hours will soften them, making the seeds easier to crack.

Finches

The information on canaries can be applied to finches.

Budgerigars

Sexing Your Bird

It *helps* to have a mature male and female budgie. In fact, things work better if you have two pairs. Budgerigars like to mate in the presence of another pair. You can't tell the players without a scorecard. Mature male budgies have blue ceres, and mature females have pink or brown ones. Budgerigars can be bred any time of the year, although spring is best.

The Nest

Nesting boxes are commercially available or can be made at home. Budgerigars are not enthusiastic about nesting material, but they may like a little dried grass or wood chips. A bare wooden floor, concaved to hold the eggs, offers the best nesting area.

Egg Sitting

Budgerigars lay four to six eggs, at intervals of two days.

The New Arrivals

The new babies hatch out in about eighteen days. Mother feeds the little ones "crop milk," a protein-rich secretion from the stomach (proventriculus), for the first few days. This is mixed with food as feeding continues. After about two weeks, father begins sharing the feeding duties. There are commercially available nesting foods that the parents can feed to their babies. You can add other soft foods such as bread soaked in boiled milk, softened seeds that have been soaked for twenty-four hours, or the yolk of a hard-boiled egg. Of course, continue feeding the parents their normal diet.

The babies' eyes will open in eight to ten days, and the down feathers will start to grow. The feathering is complete enough in a month for the babies to fly.

Weaning

Your birds can be separated from their parents at about five to six weeks of age.

Lovebirds

Do you really have a male and a female? Lovebirds can fool you. Many times a "couple" will turn out to be of the same sex, since there are no distinct physical characteristics that indicate whether a lovebird is male or female. Sometimes the behavior of the pair will "let the cat out of the bag." They will preen each other and just seem to be "in love." It is best to wait until your birds are about one year of age before breeding. The mating season is all year.

The Breeding Cage

The breeding cage should be roomy. The wood nestbox designed for the budgerigar is fine for the lovebird "delivery room." The nesting materials they like are straw, palm fronds, dried grass, and tree branches (with the bark) from fruit trees that have not been sprayed with insecticides.

Egg Sitting

Lovebirds produce a clutch of four to seven white eggs. The incubation period is eighteen to twenty-four days. Mother usually sits on the eggs. Father helps out in the feeding after the babies hatch.

Weaning

The babies are ready to leave the nest and be on their own at five to six weeks of age.

Cockatiels

Sexing Your Bird
Mature male cockatiels (those over six months old) often have bright yellow heads with orange cheek patches, although cockatiels are now seen in many color varieties. Mature males have solid grey vertical tail feathers, while females and young birds have yellow and grey horizontal barring. The breeding season is all year, although the spring and fall are best.

The Breeding Cage and Nest Box
The breeding cage should be roomy. Wooden commercial nest boxes are available in pet stores.

Cockatiels are not particular about nesting material. Wood chips or dried grass may be given to the breeding pair.

Egg Sitting and Weaning

Mother will lay three to six eggs to a clutch. They will be laid every other day. The incubation period is eighteen to twenty days. Mother and father will take turns sitting on the eggs. The babies are ready to leave the nest at five to six weeks.

The Large Parrots
(African Greys, Amazons, Macaws, and Cockatoos)

Breeding large parrots in captivity is difficult, but with the proper environment, good nutrition, and *patience,* you may be successful. Communicate with other breeders and share your information with them.

Sexing Your Birds

The most reliable way of determining the sex of the larger parrots is by endoscopy. Your veterinarian will anesthetize your bird and pass an endoscope (a tube with a light source) through a small incision in the abdomen. The sex glands will be visible. This is one way to find out if your parrot named Harry is truly a *Harry* or a *Harriet!*

In an aviary situation, the birds may pair off. This does not always mean that the pairs are of the opposite sex or that they will breed! If you *think* that you have a breeding pair, separate them from the other birds and give them their own nesting box.

The Breeding Cage and Nesting Box

The larger parrots need a very roomy aviary for their "dating."

In the wild, the larger parrots like to use old decayed tree trunks for their nesting boxes. Wooden barrels, rotting logs, or even metal trash cans can be made into nesting boxes. A wooden perch should be attached to the outside. Cut a hole large enough for the parents to enter about three to twelve inches from the top of the nesting box. Cut some ventilation holes on the sides and bottom. Attach wire mesh to the inside of the box to make it easier for the birds to climb in and out. Wood shavings and peat moss make good nesting materials. The nest box should be placed high in the aviary.

Egg Sitting

Most of the larger parrots lay two to four eggs in a clutch. The incubation period is from twenty-four to thirty days. Both parents-to-be take turns on the nest. Be sure to provide water baths, since parrots like to bathe during egg sitting. The moisture may also be needed for the developing eggs.

Weaning
The babies leave the nest at about eight to ten weeks, although the parents will still feed them for another three to seven weeks. They are on their own at about fifteen weeks of age.

SEX PROBLEMS

Sometimes birds have sex problems and difficulty "conceiving," just like all other living creatures. Consult with your avian veterinarian. He or she is very knowledgeable about preventive medicine, breeding, and reproductive health.

Common Mating Difficulties

Mating Does Not Occur • The most common causes of mating failure are that the birds are too young or too old, or that the birds are of the *same sex!* The feathers, skin, and reproductive tract are the first to suffer if birds are on an improper diet. Breeding birds need adequate space, proper placement of the nest, correct temperature and lighting, and freedom from noise and disturbances. Try changing the location of the nest if your birds are having difficulties. Various diseases and medical problems such as infections can also affect mating. Some birds just don't like each other—just as happens with humans, dogs, and cats. A bird does not *have* to be attracted to *every* bird of the opposite sex.

Select your breeding stock from domestically bred and raised birds. Progressive aviculturists evaluate their adult birds for disease or reproductive problems. Before mating, consult with your avian veterinarian.

Allow the birds to form their own pair bonds if you have enough birds of that species. You know that you have pair bonds when the birds sit close, preen each other, and keep others away.

Mating Occurs but No Eggs Are Laid • Most of the reasons just discussed are applicable.

Only Infertile Eggs Are Laid • You can "candle" the eggs. If you hold an egg up to a bright light, a red streak will indicate if they are fertile. Single hens or even those "paired" with another hen can lay eggs. Of course, these will not be fertile. Poor nutrition is an important cause of breeding problems. Sometimes age, excessive breeding, reproductive tract defects, or diseases will cause infertile eggs to be laid.

Fertile Eggs Are Laid but Do Not Hatch • Poor nutrition and chilling of the eggs are probably the major causes. Sometimes bacterial or viral infections affect the fertile egg. Be sure that there is adequate humidity. This can just be a bath provided for the egg sitters.

Eggs Are Broken • Poor nutrition may produce thin-shelled eggs. Sometimes the egg-sitting parents may be frightened and may sit too hard. This is especially true of "first timers."

Eggs Are Eaten • If one of the parents is an egg eater, it must be separated from the eggs during the incubation period. The cause of this problem is not known.

Chicks Die within Shell • The causes are not known, although poor nutrition, chilling, viruses (herpes virus), or bacteria may be important factors. Be sure that there is adequate humidity near the eggs.

EGG-LAYING PROBLEMS

In general, your assistance shouldn't be required, but be on the lookout for egg-laying problems.

Sometimes your bird may retain an egg ("egg binding"). This is more common in finches, budgerigars, and cockatiels. Your bird may be depressed and weak, and she may strain and squat in a penguinlike position. There may be blood in the droppings and a swelling of the lower abdomen. The cause is not known, although many factors may contribute to egg retention: lack of exercise, calcium deficiency, stress (especially if this is the first egg laying or if she was bred too young).

Female birds are also prone to hernias. The straining of egg laying may weaken the muscle walls. The hernia is usually located below the vent (in the lower abdomen).

On occasion, female birds may strain so hard while egg laying that the oviduct will appear as a red mass protruding from the vent. This is called a *prolapse* of the oviduct. Immediate replacement or removal is important.

Home Treatment

If your bird is having problems laying an egg, there are a few home remedies that may help. It is helpful to keep your bird in a warm (eighty-five to ninety degrees Fahrenheit) environment. A 100-watt bulb or heat lamp can be used. A few drops of warm mineral oil placed in the cloaca may lubricate the egg and ease its passage.

What to Expect at the Veterinarian's Office

Your veterinarian can diagnose egg binding by gentle palpation of the abdomen and an X-ray if necessary. Injections of calcium and stimulants of the female tubes may be considered. If the egg is visible through the cloaca, your doctor may be able to remove it with some lubrication and gentle manipulation with forceps. Anesthesia may be required. If the egg is higher in the female tube, surgery may be needed, and the chance of complications will increase. If the egg is ectopic (outside of the uterus but in the abdomen) a hysterectomy is performed. The egg material is removed and the uterus is repaired or removed.

Sometimes egg-yolk material will escape from the female tubes into the abdomen. This will cause *egg peritonitis*—irritation, swelling of the abdomen, and labored breathing. Diagnosis is made by X-ray and/or by aspirating (withdrawing with a syringe) yellowish or brownish material from the abdomen. If signs have been noticed early, the doctor may be able to save your bird's life by flushing and draining the abdomen and by giving injections of testosterone to stop egg production. A hysterectomy may be recommended, especially in chronic egg layers.

Hernias should be repaired surgically so that the intestines or other organs do not get trapped and injured in the sac.

A prolapsed oviduct usually can be cleaned off and pushed back into the abdomen with a lubricated thermometer. A few stitches are placed in the cloaca for a few days to hold the oviduct in. Sometimes if the oviduct is severely damaged, it must be surgically removed, which increases the risk to your bird.

Uterine infections are treated by a hysterectomy. Usually, a generalized infection that also involves the liver and/or air sacs is present. Antibiotics, laboratory tests, and supportive care are needed before surgery.

Are any of the following signs present?
- Sudden lethargy, depression
- Labored breathing
- Bleeding from the vent
- Swelling above or below the vent
- Red mass protruding from the vent
- Constant squatting, straining in a penguinlike style

Yes → See veterinarian NOW

No ↓

Follow home treatment

BIRD PEDIATRICS

Usually the nestling period is pleasant for all concerned—mother, father, babies, and you. But you do have a few important jobs during this time: watching for signs of illness and watching for "baby abuse" or neglect. You might consider hand raising the babies.

The yolk sac is usually drawn into the abdomen before hatching. The "belly button" is prone to infection, so swab it with a dilute povidone-iodine solution (Betadine)—and keep the chicks in a clean area.

Parent-reared birds have a sterile gut at hatching, because they receive the "good bacteria" from regurgitated crop contents of the parents. Artificially incubated and hand-raised babies can receive a fresh supply of bacteria from a donor bird of the same species. The crop contents of the donor should be examined for any "bad" bacteria or yeasts before feeding. Talk to your avian veterinarian.

Parent-reared birds must be watched carefully. They are most vulnerable to illness and other problems during the first week of life, when fledging (leaving the nest) and at weaning.

Mother and father may refuse to feed the babies if they are inexperienced parents, if the weather is too hot or too cold to stay in the nest, or if there is too much noise or activity around the nest. The chick must interact with the parents in order to be fed, so if it is ill or hypothermic (not kept warm), it will be abandoned. Sometimes the larger, stronger nestlings will be fed and not the smaller ones. Hand raising may be necessary.

Home Treatment

Some mothers may pluck their nestling's feathers—perhaps to get ready for the "next nest." If the feather picking is severe, remove the mother and let the father feed the babies or hand feed them yourself.

Sometimes because of poor hygiene, the babies' feet get encrusted with dirt. Gently washing the legs and feet with soap and water will help.

Birds prefer to feed their nestlings moist, soft foods. The adults' normal diet (moistened) and some of the hand-raising formulas are good. Feeding a poor diet or inadequate amounts to the parents will cause them to stuff anything into their demanding babies—nestling material, pieces of the perch, or other undigestible material.

If mother and father refuse to feed any of the babies, you will have to hand feed them or foster them to other parents.

Panting nestlings with wings outstretched are too hot. Move them to a cooler spot.

Check the nestlings daily.

What to Expect at the Veterinarian's Office

Sick baby birds are dehydrated, have a low body temperature (hypothermic), and have a low blood sugar (hypoglycemic). Your veterinarian will warm them to 95 to 100 degrees Fahrenheit in an incubator or with a heat lamp. Give intravenous or subcutaneous fluids containing glucose (sugar). Antibiotics and

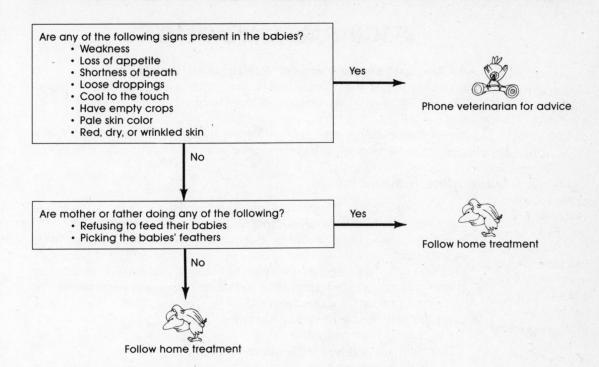

Are any of the following signs present in the babies?
- Weakness
- Loss of appetite
- Shortness of breath
- Loose droppings
- Cool to the touch
- Have empty crops
- Pale skin color
- Red, dry, or wrinkled skin

Yes → Phone veterinarian for advice

No

Are mother or father doing any of the following?
- Refusing to feed their babies
- Picking the babies' feathers

Yes → Follow home treatment

No

Follow home treatment

---

corticosteroids may also be administered. Your avian veterinarian may have you continue treatment at home.

Your veterinarian may want to do a culture and sensitivity to see if a bacterial or yeast infection (very common in baby birds) is present. Viral diseases such as pox (page 71) or papovavirus are seen sometimes in baby birds. Papovavirus, also called budgerigar fledgling disease, causes the baby birds to have a swollen abdomen, severe dehydration, no down feathers on back and abdomen, and other abnormal feathering. Many of these baby birds will die at twenty to sixty days of age, whereas others will have a chronic form of the disease: abnormal feathering, subnormal weight, secondary yeast (candida) infections, watery droppings (the urine part), and kidney failure.

AVICULTURE MANAGEMENT

Aviculture is the art and science of maintaining and breeding bird collections.

The poultry industry has flourished because it incorporates *preventive medicine* and *good hygiene* in its operation. Veterinary advice and evaluation are important.

Many of the problems seen in aviaries are related to poor husbandry. The keys to aviculture success are quarantine, good aviary design, and good hygiene.

Quarantine Rules

- Noisy species should be separate from shyer birds.
- Buy your birds from a reputable source. Ask your avian veterinarian.
- Newly purchased birds should be isolated from your other birds for thirty to sixty days.
- Feed and clean the cages of the quarantined birds last and wear different clothes and shoes. Wash thoroughly and disinfect your apparel before you enter your permanent collection.
- Carry out appropriate medical procedures.
    Weigh and perform physical exam
    Do chlamydia and Newcastle disease tests
    Do fecal, culture, and giardia test
    Deworm
    Dust feathers with 5 percent carbaryl powder
    Perform other tests as recommended by your avian veterinarian

Flight-Cage Design

- Use welded wire cages that are suspended three to four feet from a *concrete* floor. There is less chance of diseases developing, because uneaten food and feces fall through the bottom of such cages. Concrete flooring discourages rodents from digging into the bird room, and it is easy to clean.
- Use natural branches of fruit woods, eucalyptus, or nut trees for perches.
- Provide climbing and chewing activities.
- If the birds fight over the *highest* perch, place the perches at the same level.
- Food and water bowls should be easy to clean—stainless steel, plastic, or crockery. They should be placed off the cage floor and away from perches so that feces will not fall into them. You should be able to service the food and water bowls from the outside of the cage.
- Nest boxes should be watertight or protected from the rain. There should be a ladder inside deep nest boxes and a sliding trap door on the back of

the nest box to make it easier to inspect its contents and remove any birds for medical treatment.

- Your avian veterinarian can help you set up a home hospital (see page 98) for your aviary.

Hygiene

- Fresh food—fruits, vegetables, sprouted seed, or rained-upon seed—should be left in the cage for no longer than twelve hours. Bacteria, especially the gram negative type, proliferate.
- All utensils are good sources of bacteria. Utensils and appliances (such as blenders) should be scrubbed with detergent and disinfected after use.
- Collect drinking water from the tap, not from garden hoses. Let the water run for a few minutes before collection; this reduces the number of bacteria. Pseudomonas (a bad bacteria) can be isolated from garden hoses and PVC pipe.
- The nesting material must be kept dry. Aspergillosis and other fungi can cause nestling disease. Use hardwood shavings.
- You can disinfect your shoes with Environ One Stroke (CEVA Laboratories).
- Clean the food and water bowls daily. Clean and scrape the perches weekly (see "Disinfectants," page 43).
- Visitors to the aviary can bring diseases, so use the footbath. If they are fellow aviculturists, take other precautions so that diseases are not spread to their birds unknowingly. Have them wear different clothes and wash and disinfect their hands. If Newcastle disease is diagnosed in your state, do not allow any visitors to your aviary.
- Rodents can be discouraged by using a concrete floor, metal cans with tight-fitting lids for food storage, and good strong doors. Rodents spread disease organisms such as salmonella and *E. coli.* If you are having a rodent problem, talk to your avian veterinarian and pest-control specialist about the safest way to control your pest problem.

HAND RAISING BIRDS

Hand raising birds is not easy. It takes a lot of time and an "eagle-eye" watching for potential problems along the way. Keep in close communication with your avian veterinarian.

Hand-raised birds seem to be better breeders and better companions. The process can begin at hatching, although if begun at two weeks of age, the babies have received the immunity from the parents and are still adaptable to hand feeding.

The temperature of the brooding chamber should be ninety to ninety-five degrees Fahrenheit. The humidity is kept about 50 percent so that the skin does not dry out and the chick does not dehydrate.

At about two weeks of age, the temperature can be lowered to eighty or eighty-five degrees Fahrenheit. When the bird has good feathering, seventy to eighty degrees Fahrenheit is a comfortable temperature.

The flooring of the brooder is very important. Hemmed cloth diapers or indoor-outdoor carpeting works well. Sawdust or ground dry corn cobs should not be used. They can be eaten or inhaled. The corn cobs may also be a source of aspergillosis—a serious respiratory infection. Tissue paper may be too slippery. Wood (pine) shavings can be used when the birds are fully feathered.

Change and clean the nursery frequently. Food and water supplies, feeding utensils, and the brooding chamber should be kept clean and lightly disinfected.

Bird Baby Food

A diet recommended by Susan L. Clubb, D.V.M. and Kevin J. Clubb, M.S. is very good.

Ingredients

1 quart monkey biscuit
1 quart water
3 heaping teaspoons peanut butter
½ jar creamed corn baby food (4.5-oz. jar)
5 ice cubes

Directions

1. Soak the monkey biscuit in the water for 30 minutes.
2. Simmer on the stove or cook in a microwave oven for several minutes.
3. Stir in the baby food and peanut butter.
4. Cool by adding the ice cubes.

5. Mix thoroughly.
6. Test the temperature before feeding (95 to 105° F).

Make sure that it is well mixed before feeding and that the temperature is just right. If it is too hot, it will scald the crop (the holding sac in the neck). During the first forty-eight hours the diet should be 7 percent solids, then 30 percent solids until weaning. Weigh the solid and liquid ingredients separately to get the proper percentages.

Spoons, crop tubes, or catheter-tipped syringes are used for feeding. When the feeding response is displayed (head bobbing up and down), the breathing tube is closed, so that there is less of a chance of getting food in the respiratory tract.

Here are a few helpful feeding tips:

- *Amount* of food: Fill up the crop at each feeding.
- *Frequency* of feeding:
    5–6 times daily (1–5 days old)
    4–5 times daily (1–3 weeks)
    3 times daily (3 weeks and older)
    Night feedings are not necessary.
- The crop should be empty before the next feeding
- Weigh the birds daily at the same time *every day*. Lack of weight gain *daily* may be your earliest sign of illness. Contact your avian veterinarian if there is a weight loss two days in a row.
- Keep each bird in a separate box.
- Use a separate feeding utensil for each bird.
- Disinfect feeding utensils, the feeding area, and your hands between feedings.
- Isolate and feed sick birds last.

Weaning

Weaning is the time when your babies start to eat on their own. Moistening their adult diet (parrot pellets) is a good way of starting, as is leaving their feeding formula out for them to nibble.

Weaning ages for hand-raised birds are as follows:

Budgerigar—30 days
Cockatiels— 42–49 days
Conures—50–60 days
Amazon parrots—75–90 days
African grey parrots—75–90 days
Macaws—75–120 days
Cockatoos—75–120 days

Consult your avian veterinarian if you see any of the following signs:

- Weight loss two days in a row
- Red, dry, or wrinkled skin
- Sores on the feet
- Head and wing feathers developed but no body feathers growing
- Misdirected feathers on the back of the head
- Sluggishness, weakness
- Loss of appetite
- Shortness of breath
- Pale skin color
- Head large in proportion to the body
- Thin chest, feet, and toes
- Failure of the crop to empty
- Diarrhea

The most common problems seen in hand-raised birds are malnutrition and stunting syndrome; aspiration pneumonia; deviation of the legs; failure of the crop to empty; and bacterial, yeast (candida), and viral diseases. Discuss these problems—how to avoid them and how to recognize them early—with your avian veterinarian *before* breeding your birds.

Remember: Your avian veterinarian is your bird's best friend.

PART III

Wild Birds

Birds in Your Backyard

When you have a pet bird, you become more aware and interested in the birds around you. But even if you don't have your own bird, you can still feel the joy of watching birds. You can think of your yard, balcony, or terrace as an inn that will provide food and lodging for bird travelers.

Wild birds can keep you entertained for hours. They are intriguing visitors whose songs, behavior, and appearance change with the seasons. It is fascinating to observe them in their daily activities: feeding, preening, singing, courting, building nests, and raising their young. But be warned: bird watching can be addictive and hazardous to your free time!

We select our favorite inns or hotels because of the following features:

• Charm and comfort
• Convenient location
• Hospitality, safety, and security
• Dining facilities that offer consistently good food, prompt service, and predictable hours

Birds look for the same qualities in their lodgings. If you are a concerned innkeeper, you will attract many kinds of birds—and you will be able to keep them within easy watching distance for a long time.

THE RIGHT LOCATION

According to an old saying, the three most important considerations for a new business are location, location, and location. Location is also very important to birds, the ideal location having *cover* nearby.

Cover provides protection from predators. We may think of cats as the only predator that would concern birds, but avian predators such as hawks can also be a danger. *Cover* or protection consists of any sort of vegetation that will deflect the direct attack of a cat or hawk.

When attacked, birds often dive into the nearest tree or bush. Birds are attracted to out-of-the-way feeding stations close to some sort of cover—trees, bushes, hedges, or a vine-covered trellis. An appealing setting might be a corner hedge with some overhanging tree branches at the back of your yard. Ideally, visiting birds will indicate where they are most at home and comfortable in your yard. Watch where they land when they first arrive. Where do they fly when disturbed? Where do they spend most of their time? These are the areas where the feeders will be most popular.

If these locations are too far from your house or window, you might try the following:

- Once feeders are established, they can be gradually moved several feet a day until the preferred location is reached. Many of your "regulars" will follow the feeder.
- Planting additional cover at this new site will increase the comfort and attract more birds.
- By watching the birds and their movements, you will become sensitive to when and where they are the most relaxed. It takes patience and time to establish a feeding station with a faithful clientele. Experiment with different locations.
- Some people like to sit near a window while dining; others prefer a cozy corner. Birds also have their preferences. Some prefer feeding on the ground; others like to dine at higher elevations. Thus, several small feeders will prove far more effective than one large one. Such small feeders separate the birds and prevent crowding or the domination of a single feeder by one or two birds.
- Birds like to avoid nasty weather when eating or resting, so feeders should be situated in an area protected from wind and rain. If winds in your area usually come from the northwest, feeders should be placed on the south and east sides of your house.
- Since birds start their day early with a big breakfast, feeders need to be full first thing in the morning.

THE FEEDER

You can construct a variety of feeders, all of which can be made at home.

Basic Feeder • Just scatter some seeds on the ground or on a tree stump, porch railing, porch step, windowsill, window box, balcony, garden wall, or terrace.

Windowsills • Windowsill feeders can be enlarged by adding a horizontal board or shallow tray with drainage holes for the rain. An old window screen extending out horizontally from the sill also provides a good feeding surface that will not hold water. Seed should not be allowed to pile up and get moldy.

Thread or String • Bits of fruit or nuts, or even popcorn, can be strung on a thread or string and hung on a branch.

Plastic Bottles • Cut a hole in the side of a plastic bottle—two inches from the bottom. The size of the hole will determine to some extent the size of the birds that will dine from it—small hole, small birds. Birds do not need a perch on these feeders. If you do attach one, a blue jay—a bird with crude "table manners"—may sit there and throw most of the seeds on the ground. Hang the bottle from a tree or set it on your windowsill or feeding ledge—and watch the diners come!

Tree Trimmings • A branch can be made into a suet log by drilling holes in it (large holes, one inch across, if possible) and filling them with suet, cheese, or a suet–peanut butter mixture.

Cement or Cinder Blocks • Stack them on their sides and put seeds in the cores of the blocks.

Buckets and Cans • An old pail placed on its side will serve very well as a feeder until you feel that you need something fancier. Cans with plastic snap-on lids can be made into feeders: cut a small hole in the lid. Fill the can with bird seed, then hang it or place it horizontally in a tree or on a feeding station.

Other Considerations

- Make sure that the seeds in the feeders stay dry and visible.
- Provide drainage and protection from rain and snow.
- Make sure that your "patrons" are not eating moldy seed. When seed becomes moldy, bury it in your compost and clean the feeder.
- If you live in an area with heavy snow cover that lasts for more than a day or two, you can continue to attract diners by clearing the snow from some ground—a patch of lawn, garden, or compost pile—and sprinkling the area with a few seeds. Be sure to clear the ground around your feeder. This will also uncover seeds.
- Spade or turn over small sections of your garden and compost as far into the winter as possible to uncover natural grit, worms, grubs, and seeds.
- Keep in mind that a variety of commercial feeders are also available.
- *An important note:* Be a considerate host! You wouldn't invite a guest for dinner and then take away the food. Have the same consideration when feeding wild birds. Don't stop the winter feeding once you start. Your bird guests will be depending on your hospitality.
- Feeders should be at least five feet off the ground to prevent cats from leaping up into them.
- Place feeders at least ten feet away from any object that squirrels (or cats) can use to leap onto the feeder. A thirty-inch circular metal cone placed above the feeder (if it is suspended from a wire) or placed below the feeder (if it is on a feeding post) will keep squirrels from reaching the bird food.
- Glass-enclosed window-shelf feeders, with a small opening at the bottom, make it almost impossible for squirrels or other predators to have access to feeding birds. These feeders can be purchased at any hardware store.

Where to Find Feeders

Feeders and other bird supplies can be purchased at hardware stores or outdoor equipment suppliers. You may want to obtain a catalogue from the following dealers who specialize in bird feeders:

Audubon Workshop, 1501 Paddock Drive, Northbrook, IL   60062
Bower Manufacturing Company, 1021 South 10th Street, Goshen, IN   46526
Droll Yankees Inc., Mill Road, Foster, RI   02825
Duncraft, 25 South Main Street, Penacook, NH   03303
Hyde Bird Feeder Company, 56 Felton Street, Waltham, MA   02154
Wildlife Refuge, Box 987, East Lansing, MI   48823

THE MENU

To attract a varied and interesting group of patrons to your "dining room," be creative in your menu preparation and provide food that your birds enjoy eating.

- Packaged mixed seed is commercially available, as is sunflower seed. These items are usually cheaper when purchased in large quantities from seed stores rather than bought in small quantities at the grocery store.
- Try some items from your own kitchen: peanuts, suet, peanut butter–suet mix (peanut butter by itself may choke birds), cheese, hard-boiled eggs, egg shells, fruit, dried fruit, raisins, and cereal.
- Leftovers and scraps may interest birds. A stale doughnut can be hung on a branch, and bread and bread crumbs can be placed on the feeding tray. Some birds enjoy leftover turkey; winter birds like ground meat scraps (which can even be mixed with suet).
- You can arrange your plantings to provide food in a natural way for wild birds year after year. Many trees and shrubs produce seeds and berries that are high on the list of bird preferences. This vegetation will also provide cover and shelter. For suggestions, contact your local bird club, garden club, nursery, wildlife refuge, or nature center.
- Grow some bird seed in your garden. Try sunflower and corn. Dry the sunflower heads and watch the birds line up for these goodies. Be sure to avoid spraying insecticides on plants grown for bird food. If you must use an insecticide, rotenone, pyrethrin, malathion, and derris are the safest. Derris is dangerous to fish, so don't use it near a pond or stream. It is best to spray in the evening so that bees won't be killed.

How to Attract Different Types of Birds

The following list will tell you which birds may be attracted by which foods and plants.

Suet: Blue jays, starlings, chickadees, nuthatches, woodpeckers, creepers, mockingbirds, orioles, robins, sparrows, thrushes, warblers, wrens

Sunflower seeds: Cardinals, blue jays, titmice, wrens, goldfinches, chickadees, blackbirds, grackles, purple finches, and grosbeaks

Feed mixtures (millet, rape, hemp, sunflower seeds, caraway seeds): Blackbirds, cardinals, finches, goldfinches, grosbeaks, juncos, sparrows

Peanut butter (mixed with suet and corn meal): Chickadees, finches, goldfinches, blue jays, juncos, nuthatches, robins, sparrows, thrushes, warblers, woodpeckers, wrens

Plantings

Bittersweet: Catbirds, robins, bluebirds, thrushes, vireos

Blackberry: Woodpeckers, thrushes, robins, jays, titmice, mockingbirds, catbirds, thrashers, bluebirds, cedar waxwings, orioles, evening grosbeaks, goldfinches, sparrows, vireos, phoebes, warblers

Dogwood: Woodpeckers, mockingbirds, catbirds, thrashers, robins, bluebirds, thrushes, cedar waxwings, orioles, cardinals, evening grosbeaks, goldfinches, sparrows, vireos, swallows, warblers

Blueberry: Jays, chickadees, catbirds, thrashers, robins, bluebirds, thrushes, orioles, cardinals, towhees, sparrows, phoebes

Elderberry: Woodpeckers, jays, nuthatches, mockingbirds, catbirds, thrashers, bluebirds, thrushes, cedar waxwings, orioles, cardinals, evening grosbeaks, goldfinches, sparrows, starlings, vireos, wrens, phoebes, warblers

Honeysuckle: Jays, catbirds, thrashers, robins, bluebirds, thrushes, cedar waxwings, evening grosbeaks, juncos, vireos

Russian or autumn olive: Catbirds, robins, cedar waxwings, cardinals, evening grosbeaks, towhees

Bayberry: Woodpeckers, jays, mockingbirds, catbirds, thrashers, robins, bluebirds, thrushes, cedar waxwings, cardinals, purple finches, juncos, sparrows

BATHING

Birds love to bathe, just like we do. You can buy a bird bath for your birds in most garden stores, or you can design your own bath. It should be easy to clean and shallow, with fairly rough surfaces.

A garbage can lid inverted on the ground can be lined with some flat stones and filled with water. It will be more attractive to birds if you hook up a "shower" to it. An old, leaking bucket hung over a bird bath and filled once or twice a day will attract a very happy and thankful clientele.

Although we wouldn't enjoy a bathtub filled with sand, some birds would love it. This type of "bathing" probably helps keep them free of external parasites. Dry, fine dirt (sifted) and fine sand can be offered in a sandbox or raised area with good drainage. Try to place it in the sunlight with some overhead protection in case of rain.

Birds like a warm bath in the winter. If you fill your bird bath with boiling water, the birds will come to warm themselves in it when the water cools down a little.

NESTING

Birds search for *nest sites* and *nesting material* at the onset of the breeding season.

Nest Sites

Many birds like to build their nests in dense vegetation, whereas others prefer the security of tall evergreens or the branches of deciduous trees.

Robins and barn swallows may like the ledges, shelves, beams, or outdoor lights of your home, breezeway, or garage. Small nesting shelves may be used by bird guests if they are placed in protected areas. Some robins and barn swallows seem to look for heavily trafficked locations.

Nest Boxes

Cavity-nesting birds such as chickadees and wrens may use nest boxes. Dead trees left standing will provide places for woodpeckers to feed and nest. These cavities will be used by other birds in future years. The type of nest boxes that you should provide depends on your location. There are many nest-box designs available.

Nesting Material

During the nesting season, birds collect a variety of building materials. Some prefer mud for the foundation (so if it has been a dry spring, you should provide some mud for your birds); some prefer short bits of string or yarn (no longer than six to eight inches), bits of unraveled rope, burlap, or strips of rags; others may prefer cotton, lint from your clothes dryer, or animal hair (dog or horse). Clippings or brushings from your dog's no-longer-needed winter coat can be recycled by the birds to line their nests. These materials can be loosely tied or clothespinned to a bush, tree branch, or clothesline.

CARING FOR AN INJURED WILD BIRD

If you find an injured wild bird, approach it slowly and gently pick it up. (See the section on restraint in Chapter 6.)

Warmth, rest, and nutrition are the most important first aid measures for an injured bird. You can use a cardboard box lined with a towel as a "hospital." The temperature in the box can be maintained at eighty-five to ninety-five degrees Fahrenheit by using a 100-watt bulb, infrared lamp, or heating pad.

What should you feed the bird? The shape of its beak will help you determine its diet. (See the section on feeding wild birds in Chapter 3.) A bird identification book will also help you and you can call your avian veterinarian or wildlife rehabilitation center. Be sure to supply water in a container that will not tip over.

The most common cause of injuries to wild birds is flying into a window (the bird becomes confused by reflections of trees or other birds in the glass) or into wires. Should the bird merely be stunned, warmth, rest, and food may be all the medicine needed. But if a wing or a leg seems to be broken, see the appropriate Decision Chart in this book to decide what to do.

If you should find an unusual number of dead birds in a short period of time, or if you notice birds showing signs of illness (paralysis, lack of balance, unusual flight patterns), contact your veterinarian. The cause may be poisoning or some kind of virus affecting an entire flock of birds.

HELPING A BABY BIRD

If you find a naked or partially feathered baby bird, try to locate the nest. Its parents will not mind the human scent when the bird is returned to the nest, and they will usually continue to care for the nestling. You can make a new nest if you can't locate the original one. Fill a plastic berry container (with holes in the bottom so water will go through) with grass cuttings. Attach it to a tree or bush and watch for the parents to come down and feed their baby. Some young, fully feathered birds don't fly from the nest—they may just "walk" away. They will stand on the ground and cry for the parents to feed them, or they may even flutter into nearby brush. If this is the case, make sure the bird is placed in a protected bush or on a low tree limb, away from dogs, cats, and other predators.

If you cannot locate the nest or find a safe spot to leave the young bird, you'll have to feed the nestling yourself or find a licensed wildlife rehabilator recommended by your veterinarian. The following tips will be helpful:

- Warmth is of primary importance. Follow the same techniques used for an adult bird: a cardboard box lined with a soft towel, with warmth provided by a 100-watt light bulb, infrared lamp, or heating pad.
- Identify (if possible) the baby bird.
- Use a liquid diet at first (see "The Home Hospital," page 98) if the bird seems very weak.
- When the bird appears to be stronger, try a diet of canned dog or cat food, hard-boiled eggs, baby cereal, or strained baby food, as well as the above liquid diet. You can use the baby bird diet on page 202. Use a vitamin-mineral supplement.
- Baby birds should be fed every hour or two from 7 A.M. to 7 P.M. You do not have to feed them the rest of the day since birds rarely feed at night. (You might note that adult birds feed their young every fifteen minutes.)
- Tapping the side of the food container (thus imitating the sound of the parents returning to the nest) should cause the baby bird to open its mouth to be fed. If its beak does not open, *gently* press on both sides of the beak with your thumb and index finger.
- You can feed the baby bird with a dropper or by using your fingers.
- Release the bird as soon as it is fully feathered, able to fly, and readily able to eat the food you leave. You may find it difficult to release your newfound pet—but remember that wild birds rarely survive for any extended period in captivity.

FINDING EGGS

If you find eggs that have not been overly chilled, you might try to hatch them in an incubator. An insulated wooden box with a heat source may be used. Maintain a constant temperature of 103 degrees Fahrenheit; a dish of water will provide humidity in the incubator. If the eggs do not hatch on schedule, the developing bird may have already died, or the egg may have been an unfertilized one. If the eggs do hatch, your work has just begun! Baby birds that hatch fully feathered with down, eyes open, and the ability to peck for food are called *precocial.* Quail, ducks, chickens, geese, and the pheasants are in this group. Place newly hatched birds in an area heated to 85 degrees Fahrenheit, gradually reducing the heat to room temperature. A diet of "chick starter" (available at any feed store) and a bowl of water should provide adequate nutrition for the young bird.

Baby birds that are *altricial*—hatched without feathers and with closed eyes—are helpless and must be hand fed for three to four weeks. Keep them in an incubator at 95 degrees Fahrenheit the first week and 85 to 90 degrees the next three weeks. These birds can be released at five to six weeks of age. Follow the feeding formulas in this book.

GETTING INFORMATION

A particularly useful organization is the ornithological laboratory at Cornell University—available to anyone who needs information or help with bird questions. They also have excellent bird feeders, books, and recordings of bird songs available for purchase. Their address is

Laboratory of Ornithology
Cornell University
159 Sapsucker Woods Road
Ithaca, NY   14853
Telephone: (607) 256–5056

Another wonderful source of bird information is the National Audubon Society, whose many affiliated nature and bird clubs are located throughout the country. Members will be willing to help you and provide you with a list of birds to be found in your area. The society is also a good source for bird books, feeders, etc. For answers to your bird questions and the address of the nearest Audubon affiliate, write to the National Audubon Society. Their address is

National Audubon Society
950 Third Avenue
New York, NY   10022

National history museums and nature centers are also wonderful resources. They often sponsor "bird happenings," and their staff members can answer many of your questions.

Bibliography

Feeding and Attracting Birds

Dennis, John V. *A Complete Guide to Bird Feeding.* New York: Alfred A. Knopf, 1975.

Kress, Stephen W. *Audubon Society Guide to Attracting Birds.* New York: Scribner, 1985.

Bird Medicine and Care

Fowler, Murray E., editor. *Zoo and Wild Animal Medicine.* 2d ed. Philadelphia: W. B. Saunders, 1986.

Harrison, Greg and Linda. *Clinical Avian Medicine and Surgery.* Philadelphia: W. B. Saunders, 1986.

Petrak, Margaret L., ed., *Diseases of Cage and Aviary Birds.* 2d ed. Philadelphia: Lea & Febiger, 1982.

Weber, William J. *Wild Orphan Babies.* New York: Holt, Rinehart & Winston, 1978.

Bird Watching and Wild Birds

Audubon Society Staff and John Bull. *The Audubon Society Guide to North American Birds: Eastern Region.* New York: Alfred A. Knopf, 1977.

Audubon Society Staff and M. D. Udvardy. *The Audubon Society Guide to North American Birds: Western Region.* New York: Alfred A. Knopf, 1977.

Forshaw, Joseph M. *Parrots of the World.* New York: Doubleday, 1977.

Pasquier, Roger F. *Watching Birds.* Boston: Houghton Mifflin, 1980.

Peterson, Roger Tory. *A Field Guide to the Birds: A Completely New Guide to All the Birds of Eastern and Central North America.* 4th ed. Boston: Houghton Mifflin, 1980.

———. *A Field Guide to the Birds East of the Rockies.* Boston: Houghton Mifflin, 1984.

———. *A Field Guide to the Birds of Texas and Adjacent States.* Boston: Houghton Mifflin, 1979.

———. *A Field Guide to Western Birds.* Boston: Houghton Mifflin, 1972.

Robbins, Chandler S., et al. *Birds of North America.* Rev. ed. New York: Golden Books, 1983.

Stokes, Donald W. *A Guide to the Behavior of Common Birds.* Boston: Little, Brown, 1979.

Terres, John K. *Songbirds in Your Garden.* New York: Harper & Row, 1987.

Index

Reader Survey

Please take a moment to fill out this survey of bird owners.

1. What type of bird do you have? _____
2. What is its name? _____
3. How old is your bird? _____
4. Where did you find your bird?
   _____ Breeder
   _____ Pet store
   _____ Humane shelter
   _____ Friend
   Other _____
5. How many times a year do you see a veterinarian for your bird? _____
6. What other companion animals or pets do you have?
   _____ Dog
   _____ Cat
   _____ Ferret
   _____ Guinea pig
   _____ Hamster
   _____ Gerbil
   _____ Mouse or rat
   _____ Rabbit
   _____ Snake
   _____ Iguana or other lizard
   _____ Tortoise
   _____ Fish
   Other _____

7. How did you find out about *The Bird Care Book*?
　　　_____ Saw it in a bookstore
　　　_____ Recommended by a veterinarian or pet-store owner
　　　_____ Read about it in an article
　　　　　(Where was the article? _____)
　　　_____ Saw it in an advertisement
　　　　　(Where was the advertisement? _____)
　　　_____ Heard Dr. Gerstenfeld on radio or television
　　　　　(Where did you hear him? _____)
　　　_____ Given to me by a friend
　　　　　Other _____

8. What parts of this book have you found most helpful? _____
_____

9. What would you like to read more information on? _____
_____

10. Have you read Dr. Gerstenfeld's other books?
　　　_____ *The Dog Care Book* (formerly *Taking Care of Your Dog*)
　　　_____ *The Cat Care Book* (formerly *Taking Care of Your Cat*)

11. Would you like to read a book about another type of companion animal? What type? _____

12. Would you like to be on Dr. Gerstenfeld's mailing list for booklets, newsletters, or notices about new products? If so, please include your name and address with this survey.

Please mail your completed survey to:

Sheldon L. Gerstenfeld, V.M.D.
Chestnut Hill Veterinary Hospital/Bird Clinic
Market Square
Philadelphia, PA　19118

Thank You!

Would you like to talk to Dr. Gerstenfeld about your bird or other pets—dogs, cats, rabbits, guinea pigs, ferrets, snakes and other reptiles, amphibians, fish, or other creatures great and small?

- Medical problems
- Behavior problems
- Consultation before purchasing
- Sources for purchasing healthy animals

Call Dr. Gerstenfeld's help line to set up a telephone appointment:

Telephone: (215) 242-3655

Dr. Gerstenfeld will return your call at a convenient time to discuss your question. His time can be charged by Visa or MasterCard.

You may enjoy these other fine titles by Dr. Gerstenfeld, also newly revised and updated:

The Cat Care Book (Addison-Wesley), 1988
   (formerly *Taking Care of Your Cat*)
The Dog Care Book (Addison-Wesley), 1988
   (formerly *Taking Care of Your Dog*)

Addison-Wesley books are available at special discounts for bulk purchases for sales promotions, premiums, fund raising, or educational use. For details, contact:

Special Sales Department
Addison-Wesley Publishing Company
Route 128
Reading, MA   01867
(617) 944–3700